Elías Nar

Elías Nandino:
Selected Poems,
in Spanish and English

Translated and with
an introduction by
DON CELLINI

McFarland & Company, Inc., Publishers
Jefferson, North Carolina, and London

Frontispiece: Professional portrait dated 1960 when Nandino was at the height of his medical career. Courtesy Casa de la Poesía, Cocula, Jalisco, México

Selections used by permission of the Estate of Elías Nandino. Spanish texts © Estate of Elías Nandino

LIBRARY OF CONGRESS CATALOGUING-IN-PUBLICATION DATA

Nandino, Elías, 1900–
   [Poems. English & Spanish. Selections]
Elías Nandino : selected poems, in Spanish and English / translated and with an introduction by Don Cellini.
     p.   cm.
   Includes bibliographical references and index.

   ISBN 978-0-7864-4905-7
   softcover : 50# alkaline paper ∞

   1. Nandino, Elías, 1900– — Translations into English.
I. Cellini, Donald E. II. Title.
PQ7297.N23A613   2010
861'.64 — dc22   2010010903

British Library cataloguing data are available

Cover image: Elías Nandino, circa 1931. Courtesy Casa de la Poesía.

Manufactured in the United States of America

McFarland & Company, Inc., Publishers
  Box 611, Jefferson, North Carolina 28640
  www.mcfarlandpub.com

Nothing is more mine
than the sea
when I gaze out on it.
        —ELÍAS NANDINO

Acknowledgments

Thanks are due to several people who made this work possible:

In Mexico, *gracias* to Mr. Jaime Hernández Moreno, Director of Casa de la Poesía, Cocula, Jalisco — Nandino's former home, now library and museum — for access to unpublished works and photographs of the poet; to Arquitecto Daniel Montelongo Aguayo, President of the Association Ciclos Terrenales, a group that promotes the work of Dr. Nandino; to José Miguel Caravantes Ibarra, Executor of the Estate of Elías Nandino; to Dr. Javier Nandino, great-nephew of the poet, for sharing family stories; and to Ciprián Aguilar, and José Ruiz, long-time residents of the area, for sharing personal recollections about the poet. The poem "Inmortalidad del Comandante Guevara" was never included in any of Nandino's books; I am grateful to Gerardo Bustamante Bermudéz, Mexico, D.F., for locating this poem and providing the text to me. Finally, to Hector Herrera, Monterrey, for suggesting this project several years ago.

Mil gracias to Francisco Aragón and Amanda Powell for their generous lessons on translation and insightful suggestions on these poems.

Closer to home, thanks to the many friends, colleagues and former colleagues who provided encouragement and helpful feedback on various poems in this collection: Kristin Abraham, Jeff Ball, Cindy Bily, Amy Campbell, Idalí Feliciano, Diane Kendig, Dr. Dick Koch, Beth Myers and Dr. Angela Salas.

Appreciation is also offered to the Faculty Research Committee at Adrian College which provided funding to travel to Cocula in order to carry out this project.

Finally, thank you to Liz Fortini, editor of LanguageandCulture.net, where these translations originally appeared: "Si hubieras sido tú/If It Was You," "Luciérnagas/ Fireflies" and "En una noche/One night."

The following poems and translations appeared in the electronic chapbook *Like This Blind Dust: Poems by Elías Nandino*, also published by LanguageandCulture.net: "El poema inasible/ Out-of-Reach Poem," Mi primer amor/ My First Love," "Nocturna suma/ Nocturne: *Summa*," "Dentro de mi/ Inside of Me." "Autodefensa/ Self Defense," "Pre-meditación/ Pre-Meditated," "Cuando las campanas/ When the Bells," Decimas del recuerdo/ Poems of Remembering." "Decimas para un poeta difunto/ Poems for a Deceased Poet," "Tengo miedo/ I Am Afraid," and "Algún día/ Someday."

Table of Contents

TABLE OF CONTENTS

Table of Contents

Preface

In 2008, Mexican poet Jorge Esquinca released his book *Elías Nandino: El azul es el verde que se aleja*, hailed as the definitive anthology of poetry by Dr. Elías Nadino. Esquinca, now a well-known literary figure, is a former student of Nandino's. He wrote the introduction to Nandino's *El costumbre de morir a diario* and he promised Nandino that he would compile an anthology of Nandino's best poems. He has now fulfilled that promise and it is an impressive work.

This book, *Elias Nandino: Selected Poems*, takes a much different approach. Where Esquinca attempted to collect the best of the author, I have tried to provide the reader with translations of a broad overview of Nandino's poetry. Certainly, it contains many of the poems included in *El azul es el verde que se aleja*, but it includes a cross-section of his work from early poems through his mature period and even poems published just before his death at age 93. This selection traces the trajectory of Nandino's writing across his long and prolific life as a poet. It includes many of his best poems, but many others as well.

In order to help the reader understand his life-work, the poems here are arranged chronologically. Throughout his literary career, Nandino was known to often return to earlier works for revisions, sometimes changing a word or two, sometimes making significant changes. In deciding which version to include here, I have followed the lead of Sandro Cohen. In his *Antología poetica*, 1924–1982, Cohen notes this tendency of Nandino to re-work poems. Cohen maintains that frequently, Nandino worked them until they had lost much of their initial spontaneity and charm. Because of that, Cohen chose to always use the first published version of the poems in his anthology. I have followed the same pattern here, except where noted.

1

Although well-known in Mexico, particularly for his association with the Contemporáneos group, Nandino is largely unknown to readers in the United States, in part due to the fact that, to date, no translations of his work have been available. I began this project for precisely that reason, to help make U.S. readers aware of the life and poetry of this Mexican writer.

Elías Nandino died in 1993, before I had ever heard his name or had an opportunity to meet him in person. Through my reading and through the translation of his poems, however, I sensed that I had come to know him well. When I traveled to Mexico and met people who had known him personally, I came to know him even better.

His former students talked about his generosity with his time not only helping them with their writing, but inviting them to accompany him to literary events to which they would otherwise not have had access. They always mentioned the valuable encouragement he provided them.

Nandino retired from his practice of medicine in Mexico City to Cocula, his hometown, and people there also talked about his generosity, about things he had given them — furniture, dishes, and silverware from his own home — when they announced they were getting married, for example. He gave one of his suits to a young man to wear at the man's university graduation. Medical students were given his medical equipment and supplies until, little by little, he had given everything away. Each afternoon he met elementary students on the sidewalk in front of his home and talked with them about school, encouraged them to study, and gave candy to those who had done well that day.

One man from Cocula related the following event from his adolescence. Every afternoon when school was over he would go to Dr. Nandino's home. The door was always open and he would just walk in. One day, however, no one seemed to be there. He ran up to the second floor to check and, at the top of the stairs, Dr. Nandino stopped him with a gesture.

It seems that a bricklayer in town had injured himself on the job but had not sought medical attention due to lack of funds. Over time his foot became severely infected and swollen and he went to Dr. Nandino for treatment. Nandino, former physician to the stars in Mexico City, former chief of surgery at a major hospital, former winner of the national prize for poetry, was on the floor soaking the man's foot in a basin. Then he gently dried the man's foot, applied an ointment, wrapped it in a bandage and helped the man put on his sandal. When he asked Dr. Nandino how much he owed, Nandino said, "No charge and if it doesn't heal soon, come back and see me again."

When he died, Nandino left his house, his library, and his entire estate to the town of Cocula. His property is now the public library and his archives and museum are contained on the second floor of his former home.

Through my work on this book, I have come to appreciate Nandino, the man, as much as I had initially appreciated Nandino the poet. It is my hope that, through these translations, others will come to know and value his work and his life as well.

Introduction

Cocula is a small, provincial town in the state of Jalisco, about an hour's drive from the state capital, Guadalajara. Although many modern conveniences such as Internet access are available there today, Cocula still retains much of its original appearance: historic buildings line the streets and the central plaza remains the heart of town. Automobiles are the primary means of transportation, but horses are still used in town and in the country. Many roads are unpaved. In the central plaza, between the church and city hall, stands a life-size statue of Dr. Elías Nandino Vallarta, Cocula's most famous son. Born there in 1900, Nandino retired to Cocula after a career as a respected physician and poet in Mexico City. On his death in 1993, he left his furnished home, complete library, and the rights to his literary output to his hometown.

The Physician-Poet

As a child, Nandino attended elementary school in Cocula. The Mexican Revolution forced Nandino and his family to relocate temporarily to Guadalajara where he completed his secondary studies in 1915 followed by his return to Cocula (Nandino 45).

After several unsuccessful attempts at employment, Nandino eventually returned to Guadalajara, completed *preparatorio* (college-prep school, a prerequisite for admission to a university) and enrolled in medical school in 1921 (Nandino 51). During his time in Guadalajara, Nandino wrote his first formal poetry, which was published in *Bohemia* (Aguilar 66). It was at this time that Nandino made a conscious decision to pursue both poetry and medicine. He had already written *Canciones* (Songs), and his

The plaza in Cocula retains much of the charm of Nandino's time. The parish church in the background and the bandstand both appear in his novela *El Coronelito*, 1991.

work *Color de ausencia* (Color of Absence) was nearly completed (Aguilar 68).

After finishing his first year of medical school, Nandino moved again at the invitation of a friend, this time to Mexico City where he continued his studies in 1923. He loved the city and was able to lose himself in the city just "as a tree does in the forest" (Aguilar 73). In addition to his medical studies, he was able to immerse himself in the literary environment of Mexico City. Among his early acquaintances were the poets Salvador Novo and Xavier Villaurrutia (Aguilar 72). Villaurrutia would become Nandino's closest friend for the next 26 years (Aguilar 227). Between 1924 and 1928 Nandino completed his book *Espiral* (Spiral), which was published by Universidad Nacional Autónoma de México (UNAM).

During this same period, Nandino became associated with the literary group Contemporáneos, which included both Novo and Villaurrutia as well as others. This group — the famous "group without a group" — remained active until 1931 (Nandino 61). Because of his medical studies, however, Nandino was less active in this group than others and he was out of the country in 1928 when the literary journal *Contemporáneos* was published (Nandino 63). Like many other members of the Contemporáneos, Nandino was openly gay (Aguilar 195; Foster 281). Nevertheless, through careful discretion, he managed to establish and maintain a successful medical career in Mexico City following the completion of his studies at UNAM in 1930.

Nandino thus began a long and successful career as physician and poet. He lived and worked in Mexico City until his retirement in 1972, when he returned to Guadalajara and finally to Cocula. He practiced surgery at the *Hospital Juárez* for over twenty years, and was later in charge of medical services at the *Penitenciaría del Districto Federal*. He also maintained a private practice, serving many of Mexico City's literary and artistic talents such as Dolores del Río, Yolanda Montes "Tangolete" and Celia Cruz (Saavedra García 46).

Espiral, published by Imprenta Eureka in 1929, was one of Nandino's early works and includes the well-known poem "Autodefensa."

Throughout his life, Nandino was well aware that medicine and poetry have a symbiotic relationship because both deal with the mental and physical aspects of being human:

> *Para mí, sería imposible separar la vida del poeta y la del cirujano, debido a que, al mismo tiempo, los dos han participado vital y emocionalmente, en cuerpo y alma, tanto en los trágicos momentos del acto quirúrgico, como en el martirio pensante de la creación del poema.* For me, it would be impossible to separate the life of the poet and that of the surgeon due to the fact that the two have

7

participated vitally and emotionally, body and soul, at the same time in the tragic moments of surgery as well as in the pensive ordeal of creating of a poem [Encarnación 138].

Nandino's close friend Xavier Villaurrutia often accompanied him on rounds in the *Hospital Juárez*. Nandino maintained that this helped Villaurrutia become more human, more sympathetic to human suffering (Aguilar 139). Villaurrutia's unexpected death in 1950 had a powerful influence on Nandino's poetry (Aguilar 231). *Triangulo de silencios* (1953, Triangle of Silences), confronts issues of religious doubt. *Noctura palabra* (1960, Nocturne Word) shows Nandino at the height of his literary production wrestling with themes of love, solitude, death, God (Encarnación 15).

Nandino in 1931, shortly after completing his medical studies. Courtesy Casa de la Poesía, Cocula, Jalisco, México.

The publication of *Cerca de lo lejos* (Close to Far Away) in 1979 marked a change in style for Nandino. Gone were the nocturnes for which he was most famous; gone too were the sonnets and *décimas* of his earlier work. Here Nandino presented short poems, a style he continued in *Erotismo al rojo blanco* (1983, White Heat Eroticism) and *Banquete íntimo* (1993, Intimate Banquet), his final work, in press at the time of his death, composed entirely of 3-line haiku and 5-line tanka. He acknowledged that during his public readings he noticed that people did not pay attention to longer poems, and so he intentionally turned to shorter forms and poems (Hernández). He also became less concerned about the public's awareness of his sexual orientation and more concerned with the physical disabilities that aging had brought to him (Foster 282). He revealed extensive personal information to author Enrique Aguilar, who published *Elías Nandino: Una vida no/velada* (Elías Nandino: A life novelized/not veiled) in 1986, a biography of Nandino that the poet himself later denounced as unauthorized. In response, Nandino wrote his own autobiography, *Juntando mis pasos*

Nandino at the time of the opening of his medical practice in Mexico City. Courtesy Casa de la Poesía, Cocula, Jalisco, México.

(Gathering My Steps), which was published posthumously in 2000.

In addition to his work as physician and poet, Nandino is also remembered for his work with young poets. He carried out this work by providing a voice for young writers in the journals he directed — journals such as *Allis Vivere* (1926), *México nuevo* (1939), *Estaciones* (1956–1960), *Cuadernos de Bellas Artes* (1960–1964). Nandino also sponsored literary workshops that helped launch the careers of several of Mexico's contemporary writers.

The Poet-Physician

Nandino's first exposure to poetry was as a child in elementary school in Cocula. He recalled being familiar then with the work of well-known

9

Mexican poets such as Manuel Flores and Manuel Acuña (Aguilar 65). His commitment to poetry, however, began after he left his hometown and published his first works in Guadalajara.

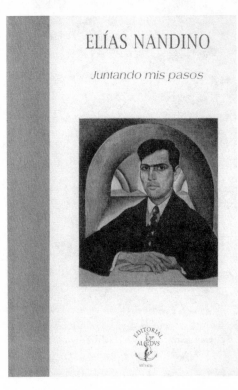

ELÍAS NANDINO

Juntando mis pasos

Nandino wrote his autobiography, *Juntando mis pasos*, in response to an unauthorized biography. The autobiography was published posthumously in 2000.

Critics have generally divided Nandino's poetic themes into contrasting pairs: life/death, faith/doubt, presence/absence (Cohen; Montenegro; Monsiváis; and Dauster). In addition to these major themes, Nandino frequently addresses issues of solitude, eroticism, and love.

The theme of life and death is so strong in Nandino's work that one book of criticism is entitled *Elías Nandino: poeta de la vida, poeta de la muerte* (Elias Nandino: Poet of Life, Poet of Death) by Mario Saavedra García. This should come as no surprise from a poet-physician who treated patients during the day and spent the evenings writing poetry in response to those experiences. He does not view life/death as beginning/end, but rather as two constants beginning before birth, accompanying one throughout life, and then reborn through death (Cohen 18). In his poem "Si hubieras sido tú" ("If It Was You," *Nocturna Suma*), a conversation with his late friend Xavier Villaurrutia, he states:

> I remember that I used to talk only
> with you about the loving siege
> that death wages against our life,
> and the two of us would talk, guessing,
> making conjectures

composing questions, inventing answers,
only to end up completely defeated,
dying in life from thinking about death.

Also included in *Nocturna Suma* is "En cada mañana" ("Every Morning")
which concludes:

And this habit of dying daily
without pain or surprise,
as natural as water
when it flows down hill,
does not let us think that we are dead
each time we sleep
but with each transitory death
our being learns
the truth of dying its eternal death.

Baptized and raised Catholic, Nandino struggled with issues of faith,
doubt, religion, and sin throughout his career. His understanding of God,
however, was not the Catholic god of his childhood. Rather, he found god
within a pantheistic view of the universe (Dauster 65). In *Poesía, Tomo II*
(1948) he writes:

I believe in you, my God
in you who are
the poetry I imagine.
Although your presence fills me,
I do not see you on a cross
but in a poem instead.

And later, in *Eternidad del Polvo*, (Eternity of Dust, 1970) he expanded
this definition to include all creation:

God is eternity
and his presence
reaches from the sky to my conscience,
and He is Everything
and I part of his life.

In his later years, the clergy of his hometown publicly denounced
Nandino from the pulpit (C. Aguilar). It was not because of his poems
about faith and doubt or because of his pantheistic view of god. Not even

his erotic poems aroused such a response from the Church as did the rhyme "*Hormiguero,*" published in 1979 ("Ant Hill," *Cerca de lo lejos*):

> The church in town
> is an ant hill
> but no one wants to say so.
> The ants arrive,
> the ants enter
> and give up every *peso*.
>
> January to December
> December to January,
> like insects drawn to honey,
> the poor ants,
> the devoted ants,
> come give up all their money.

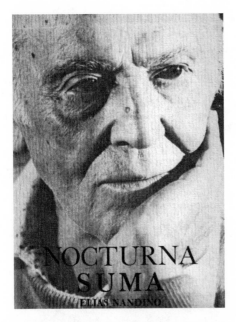

Nocturna Suma, originally published in 1955 by Editorial Muños and shown here in the 1982 edition of Editorial Katún, explores the poet's search for God.

The theme of love is often addressed in contrasting pairs of presence and absence. This is clearly expressed in "Mi primer amor" ("My First Love," *Sonetos*): "And in the blue that hides the evidence/I discover your unforgettable face,/ and suffer the presence of your absence." Included in *Erotismo al rojo blanco* (White Heat Eroticism) is the poem "Pinche Orgullo" ("Damned Pride"), in which he wrote: "I struggle with the rebellious body of your absence."

Because his love poems are not addressed to any particular individual, they have sometimes been labeled narcissistic (Cohen 22). When Nandino writes that he wants to see his beloved "like an image in a mirror," one might conclude that this label is correct. In the introduction to the

1991 edition of *Erotiso al rojo blanco* however, Carlos Monsiváis (ix) notes that the poet had long written in a codified language as he wrote about experiences which were forbidden in Mexico during Nandino's time. Perhaps what earlier critics had labeled narcissism might now suggest a desire on the part of the poet to see someone like himself, another man, in the mirror. By the time Nandino published *Erotismo*, he had publicly acknowledged that he was gay, and the publication of Enrique Aguilar's unauthorized biography, *Elías Nandino: una vida no/velada* had revealed a lifetime of intimate secrets.

Nandino is generally considered one of Mexico's masters of the sonnet form. He is also a recognized master of the *décima*, a ten-line poem of eight syllables per line with a rhyme scheme abba, ac, cddc. At the end of his career, he turned to the Japanese haiku and tanka as forms for his poems in *Banquete íntimo*. Despite his excellent technique with these forms, Nandino is perhaps best recognized for his use of the nocturne. In the introduction to his *Todos mis nocturnos,* (1988, All My Nocturnes), Nandino himself describes the nocturne as "a kind of poem that distinguishes itself by its intimate, reflexive, concentrated tone with philosophical, metaphysical and mystical tendencies, generally written at night" (19). He explains "they are born unexpectedly during our everyday occupation and then elaborate themselves in our minds until they find an echo in our deep memories." These forces join together, increasing, and on some sleepless night, at some unexpected

Published in 1989 by the City of Guadalajara, *Todos mis nocturnos* presented Nandino's previously published nocturnes in one volume.

moment, they create such an inner storm that one is forced to write the nocturne (20).

A Symbiotic Relationship

Among U.S. poets, William Carlos Williams perhaps best represents this combination of physician and poet. Among modern Mexican poets, Nandino stands out along with Enoch Cancino Casahonda and Ricardo Pérez Gallardo (Cárdenas de la Peña 84). On several occasions, Nandino described this relationship as a "precious symbiosis" (Gutiérrez López 132). "Poetry helped me understand medicine and vice versa," he stated (Aguilar 201). Indeed, it served as inspiration for much of his work.

Nandino was Chief of Medical Services at Lecumberri, the penitentiary in Mexico City, also known as the "Iron Palace." Through nineteen years of service there, Nandino learned that "the hardest of criminals has a heart and tenderness; and the best, most refined man has traces of criminality (Gutiérrez López 134). Working with inmates, whom many would consider the dregs of society, Nandino learned that everyone is capable of both good and evil. "Poetry is the knowledge of man," he commented (135).

Practicing medicine, Nandino maintained, produced in him a greater sensitivity to literature. After operating, visiting patients, prescribing medication, and spending time with friends, he would find himself writing his nocturnes in the middle of the night. In an interview with Gutiérrez López, he stated,

> "*Mis dos profesiones siempre se complementaron por que siempre me nutria de intensas emociones. Por ejemplo, puedo decirle que el contacto con el dolor humano que conocí por medio de la cirugía, me hizo tomar a la muerte como la retórica de me poesía.* My two professions complimented each other and I have always been fulfilled by intense emotions. For example, I can tell you that my contract with human suffering that I learned through surgery led me to study death as the rhetoric of my poetry" [153].

The relationship between death and poetry arose early in Nandino's writing but, after he began practicing medicine, his fascination increased. Until the very end of his own life, he continued to explore the options of death as pleasure or pain (Aguilar 139). Not only did medicine influence the themes of his work, the works themselves are filled with the language of medicine. Words such as blood, pulsing, nervous system, torso, flesh, skeleton, entrails appear frequently in Nandino's poems. Consider the opening stanzas of the nocturne "Body":

> Alone in the darkness at night,
> tired by a tiredness I don't know,
> my body collapses and gives in
> to the dark, impassive surface
> serving as support and shroud.
> I stretch out and also limit myself
> to the defenseless contour that delivers me
> to the island of oblivion where one forgets.
>
> Separated from him and submerged in him
> I remember what I have carried around all day
> like a jail of fever that oppresses me,
> like lips that speak someone else's phrases,
> like instinct that mocks my desires
> or actions out of my control;
> but seeing him like that, a bundle rendered
> indifferent in his stone-like attitude
> bronze tiger, silent pool,
> fallen column of cynicism,
> blind figure in its lesson of death;
> I perceive him as intrusive flesh
> like the ache of someone else's pain,
> accomplice on a destiny I don't understand,
> muteness that does not injure my word,
> executioner in kidnapped anesthesia.
>
> And so I feel myself divided
> and at the same time imprisoned by a mold.

Nandino seems to have captured well this affinity between poetry and medicine.

> "*Al saber la vida de los enfermos—porque ellos mismos la cuentan para explicar sus males, dicen qué hicieron, cómo y por qué; es decir, sus secretos más íntimos—uno llega a ocupar el lugar de los confesores, y toda esa información, ese conocimiento del mundo le exige a alguien con sensibilidad....* Getting to know the life of the ill — because they themselves will tell you the evil, what they've done and why they've done it — one takes on the role of confessor,

and all this information, this knowledge of the world, demands great sensitivity of the person..." [Aguilar 201].

Nandino and the "Contemporáneos"

Nandino is generally associated with the literary group "Contemporáneos." This group of young Mexican poets published a literary magazine of the same name and created a major literary movement in Mexico. This group, however, also defined itself as "a group without a group" or a "group of individuals" (Forster 7). It is no surprise therefore, that determining the membership and the years of the group's influence has proved difficult for scholars. Even a simple question such as "Was Nandino a member of the Contemporáneos?" leads to a variety of answers. Perhaps for a movement that defined itself as a group without a group, this is to be expected.

Several writers have attempted to define this group of individuals with various results. In the very title of his work *Los Contemporáneos, 1920–1932*, Merlin Forster defines the period of influence of the group. Further, in correspondence with Salvador Novo, one of the core members, Forster identifies three subgroups. The inner circle included: Bernardo Ortiz de Montellano, Enrique Gonza-

Nandino managed to outlive all the other members of the group Contemporáneos. Courtesy Casa de la Poesía, Cocula, Jalisco, México.

16

lez Rojo, José Gorostiza and Jaime Torres Bodet. The second circle was made of up Salvador Novo and Xavier Villaurrutia. Finally, Jorge Cuesta and Gilberto Owen formed the third subgroup. In addition to this core of eight poets, Forster has labeled four poets as fringe members: Carlos Pellicer, Octavio G. Barreda, Elías Nandino, and Rubén Salazar Mallén. Even further from the center, Forster includes Martín Gómez Palacio, Enrique Asúnsolo, Salomón de la Selva and Samuel Ramos.

The literary magazine *Contemporáneos* was published from 1928 to 1931, after which members went off in different directions. During the period of publication, however, Elías Nandino was continuing his medical studies in the United States and did not contribute to the magazine. Perhaps by a very strict definition, Nandino was not a member of the group.

Beranardo Ortiz de Montellano described Contemporáneos as a "group of friends" (Forster 7). Clearly, the very inner circle of members had been friends since high school and then introduced other friends to the group. In his autobiography, Nandino describes his deep friendship with Xavier Villaurrutia, and many other members of the group. As Ortiz de Montellano defined Contemporáneos, Nandino certainly was a member.

Other scholars such as José Luis Martínez (2000) include the same authors but rank their participation and influence differently. Martínez includes the original eight as noted above, but adds Carlos Pellicer as the ninth core member and fifteen more poets on the outer edge. He also defines their era of influence as 1927 to 1940.

Despite the various discrepancies in defining membership, there is agreement on the focus of the group and its publication — art for the sake of art; pure poetry, influenced by surrealism. European writers, particular French poets such as Mallarmé, Valéry, and Bremond were popular as well as Spanish poets Juan Ramón Jiménez and Antonio Machado. Writer such as Borges and Neruda, who were just beginning their literary careers at that time, were also published. Of particular note in the journal were translations of French and English writers. T.S. Eliot's "The Waste Land" as well as works by Langston Hughes, D.H. Lawrence, and William Blake were published in Spanish translation (Martínez).

In his later years, Nandino seems to have expressed some concern himself about his own place in the history of the Contemporáneos. He stated that, other than Villaurrutia, others of the group criticized his poetry and

17

viewed him has a physician who wrote poetry. Because he did not dedicate himself one hundred percent to literature, they tended to view him as a friend, as a personal physician, but not much of a poet (Gutiérrez López 84). Although Nandino always self-identified with the group, Gutiérrez López noted in an interview, that Nandino always knew sadly, that he was never fully accepted as part of that intellectual circle.

José Emilio Pacheco has stated that Nandino did not collaborate on the journal that gave name to the group only because he was specializing in surgery in the U.S. But over time we have seen that Contemporáneos is a generation, not simply a group of its most visible poets (Gutiérrez López 75).

In terms of Nandino's poetry, Sandro Cohen has identified some traits that are common to Nandino and the Contemporéneos especially with the work of Nandino's close friend Villaurrutia. Nandino himself called this influence of one on the other a type of "contamination" rather than merely "influence" (Gutiérrez López 96). Perhaps the greatest similarity is that of themes — life, death, love — however no single generation has a monopoly on these.

It is ironic that Nandino out-lived all the other members of the Contemporáneos and produced much of his best poetry long after the group had ceased to exist. Because of his longevity and his continuous literary output up until the very end of his life, he lived to see himself rediscovered. His last work, *Banquete Íntimo*, was in press at the time of his death in October 1993. Many of his early works were long out of print, but were released in new editions during the early and mid 1980s.

He was the recipient of the *Premio Nacional de Poesía de Aguascalientes* (National Prize for Poetry Aguascalientes) in 1979, the *Premio Jalisco* (Jaliso Prize) in 1981, and the *Premio Nacional de Ciencias y Artes* (National Prize for Sciences and Arts) in 1983. The *Premio Nacional de Poesía Joven Elías Nandino* (National Young Poets' Prize) is awarded annually in his honor. In his lifetime he was the recipient of some sixty recognitions and awards (Gutiérrez López 255).

Estaciones *and the literary workshops*

In addition to his work as poet, Nandino is also recognized for his work as editor and publisher. In his early years of college, Nandino organized other medical students to publish a review called *Allis Vivere* (To Live for Others) (Aguilar 73) and this was the first of several such efforts that he would make during his lifetime. He published *México Nuevo* from 1936 to 1937. In 1956, with Alfredo Hurtado Hernandez, Nandino founded a new literary journal named *Estaciones* (Seasons). One of the primary objectives of this new publication was to help in the development of young Mexican writers (Gutiérrez López 179). Indeed many established Mexican writers of today such as Elena Poniatowska published their first works in *Estaciones*. This list includes names such as José Emilio Pacheco, Carlos Monsiváis, Gustavo Sáinz, Sergio Pitol, Enriqueta Ochoa, and many other writers. It also included significant writers from Latin American and Spain.

Considered by many as Nandino's most important work, *Nocturna palabra*, 1960, explores the themes of life and death.

The journal attracted critical attention in the U.S. as well (Dauster, 1959; Carter, 1962) where it was compared in quality and stature to such publications as *Accent, Hudson Review, Prairie Schooner*, and *Shawnee Review*. These reviews also noted the importance of the journal to young writers. Carter (80) wrote that "...*el servicio más grande que la revista ha prestada a las letras patrias, resultará ser el de haber dado tanto estímulo a los jóvenes, acogiendo sus producciones y publicándolas en los suplementos bajo el título de* Ramas nuevas *y* Laberinto 14. "...the greatest service that the journal has given to Mexican letters will have to be the stimulation given to young writers, gathering their writings and publishing them in the supplements under the titles *New Branches* and *Labyrinth 14*."

In an interview, Carlos Monsiváis, who was a young writer when he worked on *Estaciones* with Nandino, stated that Nandino looked for no personal promotion, did not impose criteria, and was always available to share time, interest and attention. His attitude toward young people was very radical; he gave them the books and journals that they would need. There were none of the characteristics of a cultural impresario, but rather, a very open generosity (Gutiérrez López, 183).

In 1960, direction of the journal passed from Nandino to Gustavo Sáinz. That same year and until 1964, Nandino became responsible for *Cuadernos de Bellas Artes* (Fine Arts Notebooks) a literary publication in México, DF under the auspices of the Instituto Nacional de Bellas Artes. In 1989, with assistance from Nandino, *Estaciones nueva época* (Seasons New Era) began publication in Guadalajara under the direction of Jorge Escquinca (Gutiérrez López 181).

When Nandino retired from medicine and left Mexico City, he relocated to Guadalajara to begin the first literary workshops sponsored there by the state government. Here he also established a literary journal *Revista de Occidente* (Occidental Review), a student journal *Papeles al sol* (Papers

Elías Nandino as a young man in a undated photograph. Courtesy Casa de la Poesía, Cocula, Jalisco, México.

20

in the Sun), and published the first poetry of Ricardo Yáñez (Nandino 154). Here he continued his work with young writers including Jorge Esquinca. These workshops continued, with some interruption, until 1979 when he settled permanently in his home town of Cocula and established similar workshops there. Because of his continued dedication to helping establish young writers, the National Prize for Young Poets was named in his honor.

Out of the Closet

In both his unauthorized biography *Una vida no/velada* (Aguilar) and his autobiography *Juntando mis pasos*, published posthumously, Nandino acknowledges becoming aware of his own sexual orientation early in life (Aguilar 20; Nandino 11). In each work, "he declares, in what is now a classic twentieth-century gay tradition, that by coming out he will help dispel the mythology regarding gay sexuality and thereby contribute to the creation of a society free from prejudice and discrimination" (Ellis 107).

While serving as an altar boy for Catholic priests who traveled to remote churches to offer mass, Nandino was first initiated to homosexual activity. Throughout the remainder of his life he remained open —"but not scandalous"— about his sexuality and lifestyle (Gutiérrez López 247). His close friend Xavier Villaurrutia as well as Salvador Novo and other members of the Contemporáneos were openly gay and were publicly taunted because of it. When he was still a young man only recently having moved to Mexico City, he came to a personal acceptance of himself and describes it in his poem "Autodefensa" (Self Defense) (Nandino *Juntando*, xv):

> One day
> my conscience
> was gnawing at me
> so —
> out of desperation,
> I stood in front of the mirror
> and argued...
>
> (I left forgiven
> and both of us ended up
> crying...)

21

In his writing, however, Nandino managed to produce poems that were frequently described as "erotic" without openly identifying himself. However, beginning with *Eternidad de polvo* (Eternity of Dust, 1970) continuing with *Cerca de lo lejos* (Close to Faraway, 1979) and culminating in *Erotismo al rojo blanco* (White Heat Eroticism, 1982), Nandino began to write his way out of the literary closet as well. The poetry in these books "provides a space for Nandino to relinquish hermeticism and clarify the charged sexuality of his earlier verse. He writes freely about his homosexuality, as he comes to realize that physical degeneration resulting from aging is far more worrisome and limiting that social and moral conventions" (Pérez de Mendiola 282). It is also apparent that Nandino's early work is marked by the use of codified, self-censored language to express the "forbidden" experiences of his own sexual life (Monsivais, ix). Instead of simply stating that his poetry is often erotic, by the end of his life, it was finally clear that the work is homoerotic.

> *Esto no es asunto de valentía o cobardía; hay una imposibilidad social que determina la clandestinidad de los sonetos de Novo o García Lorca, y que influye sin duda en el tono austero enigmático de Villaurrutia o Nandino. Es altísimo el precio por sostener una disidencia erótica; a las hostilidades y burlas, hay que agregar la necesidad de un lenguaje aparentemente neutro, que elabora de continuo las vivencias más intransferibles y las ofrezca como intensidad un tanto abstracta* (Monsiváis x). It is not a matter of bravery or cowardice; there is a social impossibility that determines the clandestine nature of the sonnets of Novo or García Lorca which, without doubt, influences the austere, enigmatic tone of Villaurrutia or Nandino. There is a high price on maintaining erotic dissidence; with the hostility and taunts, one needs to adopt a language that is seemingly neutral, one that continuously describes the most personal life experiences and offers them as an intense abstraction.

The poet expresses this frustration, in the opening lines of "Poema íntimo" ("Intimate Poem" 1955):

> If I only have words and more words
> to express my anguish, my eternal thirst,
> and the words are desolate mirrors
> whose waters cannot reflect an image.
>
> If my insides feel the live chill
> of the mystery of God, which I want to express
> but the words fail me when I try
> because the idea doesn't fit and then explodes.

How can I paint the hope born in my blood,
the voice that circulates, my faraway stare,
if the words are instances of agony
transformed into echoes that die unexpectedly?

How can I sing the music of all I have dreamed,
what I see without eyes in my carnal absence
if the words are empty flower petals
impossible to save as they fall from my dreams?

How can I engrave the line of the imagined body,
the wounds of aroma that love leaves me,
if the words are errant cadavers
and it's impossible to give them a new heart?

Consider how much this codified language has changed by the publication of *Erotismo*. The earlier language of the physician is still obvious, but the veiled, coded language has given way to simple, direct expression. The poem "Eso somos" (The way we are) concludes:

That way we enjoy
everything
the clean and the dirty
the impure and the holy
which, in the end,
is how we are:
dung and dreams
modest and shameless
goodness and poison
and a pile of tendons,
arteries, intestines,
viscera and bones,
and the skin that hides
encloses, defines
and give us form.

Conclusion

The poet-physician Elías Nandino wrote about the classic themes of the human experience: life and death, doubt and faith, love and solitude. His work is generally described as accessible and unadorned. His long life allowed him to explore these themes throughout his writing career. At the

23

Elías Nandino
CERCA DE
LO LEJOS

letras mexicanas
FONDO DE CULTURA ECONOMICA

Cerca de lo lejos, 1979, showed a radical change in style for Nandino. The long, formal nocturnes had been replaced with short, free-verse poems.

conclusion of his autobiography *Juntando mis pasos* he includes a poem titled, ironically, "Poema prefácio" ("Preface Poem"), which begins:

> It does not matter to me
> how my life is judged.
> I've tried to live it
> finding exactly
> what I wanted.

Nandino spent his final years in his hometown, isolated from the very people he had returned to live among in retirement. He had outlived many friends and colleagues, including all of the former members of the Contemporáneos. Nearly deaf and blind, he lived alone, in a private world. He rose at 9:00 and retired by 6:30 in the evening, and wrote, as he pleased, in between. He ignored phone calls from Mexico City and declined all invitations to attend literary events (Hernandez). He did, in fact, live his life exactly as he wanted, writing his poems until the very end.

Works Cited

Aguilar, Ciprián. Personal interview. Cocula, Jalisco, Mexico. July 8, 2005.

Aguilar, Enrique. *Elías Nandino: una vida no/velada.* 2d ed. Mexico, DF: Océano, 2000.

Cohen, Sandro. "Prólogo" in *Elías Nandino: Antología poética 1924–1982.* Mexico, DF: Editorial Domés, 1983.

Dauster, Frank. *Ensayos sobre poesía mexicana: Asedio a los "Contemporáneos."* Mexico, DF: Ediciones de Andrea, 1965.

Encarnación, Salvador. *Elías Nandino revisitado.* Guadalajara: Secretaría de Cultura de Jalisco, 2000.

Foster, David William. *Latin American Writers on Gay and Lesbian Themes.* Westport, CT: Greenwood Press, 1994.

Gutiérrez López, Gabriela. *Elias Nandino.* Guadalajara: Secretaría de Cultura de Jalisco, 2000.

Hernández, Jaime. Personal interview. Cocula, Jalisco, Mexico. July 11, 2005.

Monsiváis, Carlos. "De los poderes menguantes y las recuperaciones irónicas" Introduction to *Erotismo al rojo blanco.* Elías Nandino. Guadalajara: Editorial Ágata, 1991.

Montelongo, Daniel. Personal interview. Cocula, Jalisco, Mexico, July 8, 2005.

Montemayor, Carlos. "El Nocturno de Elías Nandino" Introduction to *Eternidad del polvo / Nocturna palabra.* Elías Nandino. Mexico, DF: Consejo Nacional para la Cultura y las Artes, 1991.

Nandino, Elías. *Antología Poética 1924–1982.* Sandro Cohen, ed. Mexico, DF: Editorial Donés, 1983.

_____. *Banquete íntimo.* Guadalajara, Jalisco: Secretaría de Cultura de Jalisco, 1993.

_____. *Cerca de lo lejos.* In *Dos poemarios afines ... de siglo.* Guadalajara, Jalisco: Editorial Ágata, 1993.

_____. *Erotismo al rojo blanco.* 3rd. ed. Guadalajara, Jalisco: Editorial Ágata, 2001.

_____. *Eternidad del polvo / Nocturna palabra.* Mexico, DF: Consejo Nacional para la Cultura y las Artes, 1991.

_____. *Juntando mis pasos.* Mexico, DF: Editorial Aldus, 2000.

_____. *Poesía Tomo II.* Mexico, DF: Nueva Voz, 1948.

_____. *Sonetos (1937–1939).* 2nd. Ed. Mexico DF: Editorial Katún, 1983.

_____. *Todos mis nocturnos.* Guadalajara, Jalisco: Ayuntamiento de Guadalajara, 1988.

Saavedra García, Mario. *Elías Nandino: poeta de la vida, poeta de la muerte.* Guadalajara: Editorial Ágata, 1997.

The Poems

Poema Prefacio

No me importa
cómo juzguen mi vida,
yo traté de vivirla
haciendo estrictamente
lo que ella apetecía.
No hubo deseo
tentación o capricho
que no le realizara
con eficaz esmero.
Y fuera lo que fuera
al tiempo de cumplirlo
lo transformé en ensueño.

Por ella fui lascivo
y no he dejado puro
ni un poro de mi cuerpo.

Fue tal mi apego
a los desmanes
de su carnal orgía,
que a mis ochenta y dos años
de su infierno en ruinas
aún estoy creando mi poesía.

Erotismo al rojo blanco
1983

Preface Poem

It doesn't matter to me
how my life is judged.
I've tried to live it
doing exactly
what life wanted,
every desire,
temptation and whim
carefully
completed.
And, whatever it was,
when finished,
a dream had come true.

In my lust for life
not a single pore of my body
remains pure.

With such attention
to the excesses
of my carnal appetite,
at eighty-two years old,
I'm still creating my poems
from this hell in ruins.

Árbol de magnolia

Eres una jaula verde
donde duermen
blancas palomas extáticas
con el pico bajo el ala.

Espiral
1928

Mi pueblo

Un silencio "en blanco"
lastimado por la tos
de un viejo reloj
que aún no sabe contar
hasta las XXIV.

Espiral
1928

Magnolia Tree

You are a green cage
where the ecstatic
white dove sleeps,
with beak beneath its wing.

My Village

A sleepless silence
ruined by the cough
of an old clock
that still can't count
to twenty-four.

Autodefensa

Un día
la voz de la conciencia
me laceraba tanto
que, desperado,
me coloqué
frente al espejo
y discutí...

(Salí absuelto
y los dos terminamos
llorando...)

Espiral
1928

Self Defense

One day
my conscience
was gnawing at me
so —
out of desperation,
I stood in front of the mirror
and argued...

(I left forgiven
and both of us ended up
crying...)

Sobre tus ojos dormidos

Sobre tus ojos dormidos
dejo mis ojos cerrados
para dormir con tu sueño
y salir de ti, contigo,
por los remansos del aire,
por los espacios sin tiempo.

De la ausencia de las manos
brotará nueva caricia,
para rozar la intangible
presencia de nuestros cuerpos.

Un olvido de palabras
formará el idioma exacto
para entender las miradas
de nuestros ojos cerrados.

Y sin brazos que te opriman
y sin labios que te besen,
seré tu espejo en silencio
serás silencio de espejo.

Allá, en el lecho, dormidos
se quedarán nuestros cuerpos,
como niños enlazados
en un acceso de miedo...

Río de sombra
1935

On Your Sleeping Eyes

I'm resting my closed eyes
on your sleeping eyes
so I can sleep in your dream
and flee with you,
for the backwaters of air,
for timeless space.

In the absence of hands,
a new touch will spring forth
to graze the intangible
presence of our bodies.

An oblivion of words
will form a precise language
to understand the glances
of our closed eyes.

Without arms to squeeze you
without lips to kiss you,
I'll be your silent mirror
and you the mirror of silence.

Sleeping here in bed,
our bodies will be
like children huddled together
as fear approaches...

¿Por qué no soy yo tu cuerpo?

¿Por qué no soy yo tu cuerpo
sobre mi cuerpo desnudo
para abrazarme a mi tronco
y sentir, de ti, mi fuego
ascendiendo por mis muslos?

¿Por qué no soy yo tus ojos
para llorar con los míos
a la sombra de mi pecho
y romper con gotas de agua
los cristales del silencio?

¿Por qué no soy yo tus manos
para jugar con las mías
y pasando por mi cuerpo,
como juguetes de viento
inventar nuevas caricias?

¿Por qué no soy yo tu boca
para besarme en el fuego
que se despierta en mis labios
y sentir que soy yo mismo
que se vierte en otro vaso?

¿Por qué no vivo en tu vida
para sentir lo que siento,
en el fondo de tu pecho
y mirar que te me acercas
como imagen del espejo?

Quisiera ser vaso y vino,
las raíces y las ramas,
la ribera y la corriente,
la campana y el sonido,
el combustible y la llama.

Sigue durmiendo sin verme
que yo, despierto, a tu lado,
vuelo al vuelo de tu sueño
y estoy tan cerca de ti,
que respiro por tu cuerpo.

Rio de sombra
1935

36

Why Can't I Be Your Body?

Why can't I be your body
on top of my naked body
to hug myself
and feel the fire traveling
up my thighs through you?

Why can't I be your eyes
so they can cry with mine
in the shade of my chest
and crack the silence
with beads of water?

Why can't I be your hands
to play with mine
and run them across my body
like toys pushed by the wind
to invent a new caress?

Why can't I be your mouth
to kiss myself in the fire
you have sparked on my lips
and feel that I am the one
pouring himself into the other?

Why can't I live your life
to feel what I feel
deep within your chest
and watch you approaching me
like an image in the mirror?

I want to be both glass and wine,
the roots and the branches,
the riverbank and the current,
the bell and its sound,
the fuel and its flame.

Keep sleeping without seeing me,
awake here beside you.
I fly into the flight of your dream
to be so close to you
I breathe through your body.

Mi primer amor

El azul es el verde que se aleja
—verde color que mi trigal tenía—;
azul ... de un verde, preso en lejanía
del que apenas su huella se despeja.

Celeste inmensidad, donde mi queja
tiende su mudo vuelo noche y día,
para buscar el verde que tenía
verde en azul ... allá donde se aleja...

Mi angustia, en horizonte libertada,
entreabre la infinita transparencia
para traer mi verde a la mirada.

Y en el azul que esconde la evidencia
yo descubro tu faz inolvidada,
y sufro la presencia de tu ausencia.

Sonetos
1937, 1991

My First Love

Blue is green that fades away
— green, the color of my wheat field —
blue ... to green, a prisoner far away
whose memory is scarcely visible.

Immense heaven where my complaint
tends its mute flight night and day
looking for the green I had,
green into blue ... far away where it fades...

My anguish, a limitless horizon,
half opens the infinite shimmer
bringing my green into view.

And in the blue that hides the proof
I discover your unforgettable face,
and suffer the presence of your absence.

¡No sé cómo mirar para encontrarte...

¡No sé cómo mirar para encontrarte,
horizonte de amor en que me excito,
distancia sin medida donde habito
para matar las ansias de tocarte!

¡No sé cómo gritar para llamarte
en medio de mis siglos de infinito
donde nace el silencio de mi grito
movido por la sangre de buscarte!

Mirar sin que te alcance la mirada,
sangrar sin la presencia de una herida,
llamarte sin oírme la llamada;

y atado al corazón que no te olvida,
ser un muerto que tiene por morada
un cuerpo que no vive sin tu vida.

Sonetos
1937

I Don't Know How to Search for You...

I don't know how to search for you
— horizon of love which excites me,
measureless distance I inhabit —
to quell my longing to touch you!

I don't know how to scream for you
in the middle of the infinite centuries
where my silent scream is born
moved by blood to look for you!

To search without seeing you
to bleed without a wound
to call you without hearing myself;

and attached to a heart that doesn't forget,
a dead man who has as his shelter
a body that can't live without you.

Estás en mí...

Estás en mí como latido ardiente,
en mis redes de nervios temblorosos,
en mis vetas de instintos borrascosos,
y en los mares de insomnio de mi frente.

Estás fuera de mí, como vertiente
de voces imprecisas, de sollozos,
de filos de secretos tenebrosos,
y roces de caricia inexistente.

Me cubres y me encubres, sin dejarme
un espacio de ver sin tu presencia,
un átomo sin linfa de tu aliento.

Estás en mí, tocándote al tocarme,
y palpita la llama de tu esencia
hasta la hondura de mi pensamiento.

Sonetos
1939

You Are in Me...

You are in me, a fervent pulse
of my trembling nervous system,
in my veins of stormy instinct,
in the oceans of insomnia in my head.

You are outside of me, like the slope
of vague voices, of sobs,
of edges of dark secrets,
and the touch of absent caresses.

You cover and uncover me, leaving
no space without your presence,
no atom without trace of your breath.

You are in me — touching me I'm touching you.
And the flame of you pulses
in the depths of my thoughts.

Más lejos

Más lejos de la química y del odio,
de los cauces ocultos de los ecos,
del espejo nocturno de la sombra.
Más lejos...

Más lejos de los nombres y los tactos,
de las grises arañas de los pubis,
de los rojos moluscos de las lenguas.
Más lejos...

Más lejos de la voz y del pecado,
de las fuertes cadenas de la herencia,
del reloj de la edad, de la inocencia,
Más lejos...

Más lejos del pavor de las tinieblas,
del pulso luminoso de la estrella,
del grito subterráneo de la sangre.
Más lejos...

Más lejos del suplicio de los torsos,
de las aguas marinas de los besos,
de las olas azules del recuerdo.
Más lejos...

Más lejos de la cárcel del abrazo,
del eterno clamor de la esperanza,
del olor de la tierra y de las ramas
Más lejos...

Más lejos del amor y las pasiones,
del divino crisol de la impureza,
del grito interminable de la carne.
Más lejos...

Más lejos del pudor y del cinismo,
del árbol corporal que nos enrama,
de la sed insaciable que nos vence.
Más lejos...

Further

Further than chemistry and hate,
than the dark channels of echoes,
than the nocturnal mirror of shadow.
Further...

Further than the names and touches,
than the gray spider of the pubis,
than the red mollusks of tongues.
Further...

Further than voice and vice,
than strong chains of heredity,
than the clock of age, of innocence.
Further...

Further than the terror of shadows,
than the luminous pulse of stars,
than the subterranean scream of blood.
Further...

Further than the torture of torsos,
than the sea waters of kisses,
than the blue waves of remembering.
Further...

Further than the prison of embraces,
than the eternal clamor of hope,
than the smell of earth and branches.
Further...

Further than love and passions,
than the divine crucible of impurity,
than the unending scream of flesh.
Further...

Further than frankness and cynicism,
than the corporal tree surrounding around us,
than the unquenchable thirst that defeats us.
Further...

Más lejos del impulso del instinto,
del látigo invisible de la fiebre,
del sollozo que arranca mi ternura.
Más lejos...

Más lejos de la red de los sentidos,
del veneno excitante de la histeria,
de la dulce amargura de sentirnos,
Más lejos...

Más lejos yo me voy cuando te pienso,
cuando olvido tu forma de presencia
y te formo en el aire de mis sueños.
Más lejos...

Casi al cósmico borde del comienzo,
en la frente de Dios, en el convulso
malestar de la luz y del silencio.
Más lejos...

Tan lejos me distancio de mi mismo
cuando estoy a la orilla de tus ojos
que en la carera de mis pensamiento
lo olvido todo...

Tan lejos es el mundo que me inspiras,
que tengo miedo de seguir volando
por sendas de dolor y de misterio
y quedarme solo...

Es mejor que te quiera y no te piense,
cuerpo a cuerpo vencidos por la llama
del amor que encadena nuestras vidas.
Muy cerca...

Es mejor que me quede emparedado
en tu abrazo carnal que me destroza,
en tu instinto animal que me consume.
Muy cerca...

Further than the impulse of instinct,
than the invisible beating of fever,
than the sob that rips out my affection.
Further...

Further than the network of senses,
than the exciting poison of hysteria,
than the sweet bitterness we feel.
Further...

Further than where my thoughts roam
when I forget the presence of your form
and I shape you in the air of my dreams.
Further...

Almost at the cosmic border of beginning,
in the mind of God, in the disturbing
unease of light and silence.
Further...

I travel so far from myself
when I am on the shore of your eyes,
that my racing mind
forgets everything...

The world you inspire is so far away
I am afraid to keep flying
along paths of pain and mystery
for fear of being left alone...

It's better to love you and not think,
body to body conquered by the flame
of love that shackles our lives.
So close...

It's better that I stay wrapped
in your carnal embrace that overtakes me,
in your animal instinct that consumes me.
So close...

Es mejor no salir de la caricia,
del litoral de carne que nos une,
del gusto verdadero de gozarnos.
Muy cerca...

Ya no quiero evadirme de mi cuerpo,
transformar tu figura en lo que sueño
sólo quiero saber que estás conmigo.
Muy cerca...

Nudo de sombras
1941

It's better not to leave this caress,
the coast of flesh that unites us,
the true pleasure of pleasing each other.
So close...

I no longer want to escape my body,
or turn you into my dreams.
I just want to know that you're with me.
So close...

No te acerques a mi

De verdad, te quiero tanto,
que hasta de mí te defiendo.

Si arrastro lo que soy y lo llevo
por el fuerte declive del silencio
sin poder descansar con mis palabras.
Si me pesa la vida y ya no puedo
la piedra de mi historia acumulada.

Si me acerca un total remordimiento
por pecados ajenos, ignorados,
que no sé lo que son, pero que duelen
en la íntima hondura de mi mente.

Si llevo como un cúmulo de edades
hundidas en el hueco de mi cráneo,
que engendran un desfile de figuras
que van sobre mis pasos, caminando.

No te acerques a mí, tibio sollozo,
bandera musical de una esperanza;
no te acerques a mí, que soy el humo,
de humedades amargas y de arenas.

No te acerques a mí, no tengo manos,
soy trunco de caricias y de roces,
soy deshielo de nieves olvidadas,
soy un hombre sin nombre ... soy fantasma...

No te acerques a mí, porque el contagio
de mis ciegos errores, de mis traumas,
pueden matar tu cáliz aromado
y volverte agua amarga cual mi sangre...

No te acerques a mí, sigue tu vuelo,
succiona la manzana y el ensueño,
prueba el azúcar de la fruta herida
con el hambre inocente de tus ansias.

50

Don't Come Near Me

Truthfully, I love you so much
that I will defend you even from me.

If I drag myself
down the steep slope of silence
without resting with my words.
If life weighs me down and I can no longer
carry the stone of my long history.

If a complete remorse for my long-forgotten
sins approaches me,
I don't recognize them, but they ache
in the intimate depths of my mind.

If I carry a parade of figures I've conjured
like a heap of ages
sunk in the hollow of my skull
following in my steps, walking.

Don't come near me, half-hearted cry,
musical colors of hope;
Don't come near me, for I am smoke
of bitter humidity and of sand.

Don't come near me. I have no hands,
I am incapable of caresses and touching,
I am thaw of forgotten snows,
I am man without name ... I am phantom...

Don't come near me because my blind errors
and my traumas are contagious.
They can destroy your sweet-smelling vessel
and turn your blood into bitter water like my blood...

Don't come near me. Follow your flight,
taste the apple and the daydream,
savor the sweetness of the fallen fruit
with the innocent hunger of your desires.

No te acerques a mí, busca la cima
con las alas azules de tus sueños,
y alarga el brazo hasta la rama altiva
y corta el fruto de olorosa veta.

No te acerques a mí, vive tu vida,
desangra sin piedad tu adolescencia;
escala el goce de la lumbre ajena
y quema tu color en los placeres.

No te acerques a mí, porque el ocaso
que alumbra el horizonte de mi muerte,
puede manchar el himno de tu aurora
y transformarte en sombra de mi sombra...

Prismas de Sangre
1945

Don't come near me. Look for the peak
on the blue wings of your dreams,
and reach for the highest branch
to pick the sweetest of fruit.

Don't come near me. Live your own life,
leave your adolescence without looking back;
scale the enjoyment of other fires
and burn your color in their pleasure.

Don't come near me because the sunset
that lights the horizon of my death,
can tarnish the hymn of your dawn
and transform you into the shadow of my shadow...

Sonetos al desamor

I

Estás conmigo — tronco de amargura —
derramando tu savia atormentada
en mis brazos de sombra congelada
que no vive la flor de tu ternura.

Estás conmigo — infierno de locura —
temblando entre mi carne calcinada
que no siente la luz de tu mirada
ni tu tacto de punzante quemadura.

El desamor —¡la muerte que temía!—
me separa del lirio sollozante
de tu pasión que mi caricia implora.

Y presos en el nudo de agonía,
somos el eco de un amor distante
que por los dos al mismo tiempo llora.

II

¿Qué clima de dolor funde el momento
que — ayer incendio — ahora es noche fría?
¿Por qué si tu presencia era mi día
luminoso y tu beso el sacramento

que transformaba el nardo de tu aliento
en el milagro de la Eucaristía,
hoy forman un calvario de agonía
con los rigores del glacial tormento?

Ni soy yo, ni eres tú, los que juntamos
los dos temblores en sollozo inerte,
otros somos en esta cruz oculta.

El desamor borró lo que soñamos
y el nudo de las almas se convierte
en una angustia que a los dos sepulta.

Sonnets to Indifference

I

You are with me — torso of bitterness —
spilling your tormented life
in my arms of frozen shadow
where your tenderness no longer lives.

You are with me — maddening hell —
trembling beside this charred body
that does not feel the light of your look
or your sharp, burning touch.

Indifference — the death I feared —
separates me from the your sobbing passions
begging for my caress.

Prisoners in this knot of agony,
we are the echo of a distant love
and we both cry together.

II

What sad weather creates the moment —
yesterday on fire, and now a cold night?
If your presence was my luminous day
and your kiss the sacrament

that transformed the flower of your breath
into the miracle of the Eucharist,
why do they form a Calvary of agony
with the strength of a glacial storm today?

You and I are no longer what we were together.
We are someone else on this hidden cross —
trembling, lifeless, weeping.

Indifference erased what we dreamed of
and the knot of our souls has become
an anguish that buries us both.

III

Tu mano — como nube estremecida —
siembra en mi piel el roce de tu anhelo
y vierte la caricia de su cielo
en mis aguas de sangre enochecida.

Me das la brisa que en tu boca anida
y no puedo embriagar mi desconsuelo
porque tu llama incita mi deshielo
y me quema la hoguera de tu vida.

El clima de tu sueño no es el mío
y hoy no siento tu aroma de presencia
ni tu sientes mis ramas de ternura.

Nos envuelve un infierno de vacío
y somos dos pedazos de existencia
que sufren y no entienden su amargura.

Espejo de mi muerte
1945

III

Your hand — like a trembling cloud —
places your desire on my skin
and spills the caress of its sky
in my darkening waters of blood.

You give me a breeze from deep inside.
I can't get drunk on my despair
because you melt me with your flame,
you scorch me with the fire of your life.

The essence of your dream is not mine.
I don't sense the aroma of your presence;
you don't feel my limbs of tenderness.

An empty hell envelops us…
we are two pieces of existence who suffer
and don't understand their bitterness.

Poema en tu cuerpo

I

Soy joven en tu cuerpo, soy tu sangre;
el musgo de los años en tus días;
la nube de experiencia que te roza
con los sabios instantes del pecado.

Soy el nido senil donde se agita
tu forma — combustible de mi fiebre —,
que enciende la obsesión de mi deseo
por envidia al abril de tus mejillas.

Soy demonio que crece en tu sonrisa,
el cielo asesinado en tus pupilas;
la tragedia que amarga tu saliva
con el raro sabor de mis instintos.

II

Vampiro de tu savia — sed de goce —
transito por el bosque de tus ansias,
despertado la flor inesperada
que nuevo aroma a tu avidez ofrece.

En el incendio de tu carne formo
al ser imaginado en tu lujuria
y, dejo de ser yo, para entregarme
en otro cáliz que mi amor inventa.

Subo a la cumbre de tus inquietudes
para bajar, desnudos, tus pudores,
y arroparlos con hábil tacto ardiente
hasta volverlos hambre que me acose.

Y eres tú, debes ser, yo lo presiento:
el lirio humano que en mi noche expire
con el espasmo de mis agonías
y mis olas de frases amorosas...

Poem on Your Body

I

I am young in your body, I am your blood;
the moss of years in your days;
the cloud of experience that grazes you
with wise instances of sin.

I am the senile nest where your form
is shaken — fuel of my fever —
igniting the obsession of my desire
and my envy of April in your cheeks.

I am the demon who grows in your smile,
the murdered sky in your pupils;
the tragedy that makes your saliva bitter
with the strange flavor of my instincts.

II

Vampire of your sap — thirst of pleasure —
I travel through the forest of your anxieties,
waking an unexpected flower that offers
its new aroma to your greediness.

In the fire of your flesh I form myself
to the image of your lust and I cease to exist
to abandon myself
into another chalice invented by my love.

I climb the summit of your restlessness
to lower your modesties, naked,
and wrap them with a skillful, ardent touch
until they return with the hunger that hounds me.

And you are, you must be, I feel it:
the human lily who expires in my night
with the spasm of my agonies
and waves of amorous phrases...

Y eres tú, debes ser, la tumba virgen
donde entierre los restos de mis nervios:
el surco donde deje la semilla
de este pecado errante que me ahorca.

III

Quiero ser el veneno de tu entraña;
lo bueno, lo tremendo, lo imposible,
el ángel y el demonio en un abrazo;
sierpe y paloma en tu ramaje verde.

Quiero ser el cadalso de tu fuerza;
tu sombra, tu tristeza, tu fantasma;
el gustano que muerde tu memoria
y siempre te pronuncie mis palabras.

IV

Soy joven en tu cuerpo, soy tu muerte:
el espectro que vive de tu sangre;
el hombre que tus límites devora
como lobo que traga los corderos.

Pero Santo o Demonio, soy tu centro;
el amor con el odio de beberte;
el viento que desata la marea
en el desnudo mar de tu pureza.

Y tengo que vivir de tus anhelos,
sangrar tu boca, y contagiar mi sombra
en la luz infantil de lo que esperas
y en la cruda verdad de lo que gozas.

And you are, you must be, the virgin tomb
where I bury the remainder of my nerves:
the furrow where I leave the seed
of this errant sin which strangles me.

III

I want to be the poison inside you;
the good, the tremendous, the impossible,
the angel and devil in one embrace;
serpent and dove in your green branch.

I want to be the scaffold of your strength;
your shadow, your sadness, your specter;
the worm that eats your memory
and then speaks you as my words.

IV

I am young in your body, I am your death:
the specter who lives in your blood;
the man who devours your limits
like the wolf that swallows the lambs.

But, Saint or Demon, I am your center;
the love-hate of drinking you;
the wind that frees the tide
in the naked sea of your purity.

And I must live in your longings,
bloody your mouth, and infect my shadow
in the childlike view of your hopes,
the raw truth of your desires.

V

Ayúdame a existir, yo te lo pido;
quiero escalar las nubes de tus sueños,
germinar en la luz de tu cerebro
y esclavizarte con mi pensamiento.

Ayúdame a existir para quemarme
en la hoguera inocente de tu carne,
y en una llama — confundida sangre —
los dos atesorarnos en ceniza.

Poesía, Tomo II
Subtítulo "Prismas de sangre"
1949

V

Help me exist, I beg you.
I want to climb the clouds of your dreams,
take root in the light of your brain
and enslave you with my thoughts.

Help me exist, to burn myself
in the innocent bonfire of your flesh,
in a single flame — blood inseparable —
the two of us a treasure of ash.

Décimas del recuerdo
(Fragmento)

10.

Dos vidas estoy viviendo
en cada instante que pasa:
la extinguida, que me abrasa
con los recuerdos que enciendo,
y lo que voy destruyendo
al vivirla, para hacer
más recuerdos con que ver
la primera enriquecida.
De una vida hago otra vida
y las dos forman mi ser

Triángulo de silencios
1953

Poems of Remembering
(Fragment)

10.

I am living two lives
in each instant that passes:
the extinguished one that burns me
with the memories I ignite
and the one I destroy
by living it to make
more memories
to fuel the first.
From one life I create another
and the two form my being.

Décimas para un poeta difunto
(Fragmentos)

1.

A ciegas voy caminando
por la orilla silenciosa
de tu ausencia misteriosa
donde te estoy escuchando.
Yo sé que al irte buscando
acelero mi caída,
porque la lucha atrevida
de mis obstinación por verte,
es ansiar mi propia muerte
para asomarme a tu vida.

Triángulo de silencios
1953

3.

Intangible, sin figura,
flota tu nueva existencia
transparente en transparencia
infinitamente pura.
En el fondo de la hondura
de mi silencio vendado,
mi monólogo callado
habla contigo y percibe
que no has muerto porque vive
tu ardiente voz a mi lado.

Triángulo de silencios
1953

Poems for a Deceased Poet
(Fragments)

1.

I walk blindly
along the silent shore
of your mysterious absence
where I am listening to you.
I know that searching
accelerates my fall
because my stubbornness
to see you,
to make your life reappear,
hastens my own death.

3.

Intangible, your new existence
floats without form
transparent in transparency
infinitely pure.
At the bottom of the depths
of my muffled voice,
my silenced conversation
speaks with you and senses
you have not died because
your fervent voice lives beside me.

Epílogos a un poeta difunto

Tu fuga me convence que sabías
que nunca andabas solo
y que detrás del eco de tus pasos
otros pasos sin eco te seguían...

Tú supiste del goce anticipado
de morir cada día
y de poder mirar tu propia muerte,
con los ojos cerrados.

Tu palabra desnuda y palpitante
era sonido y eco,
como si ya volviera fatigado
de un lejano viaje.

Todo en ti fue la vida de tu muerte,
presentido y sentido
un coloquio de sangre y de misterio
habitando tu frente.

La temperatura de tus palabras
era llama de hielo
agua viva que en ardiente frío
la sangre penetraba.

Cortaba tu poesía como el filo
de un metal delgado
que sin herir la piel hería la entraña
con su tacto frío.

Pureza pura, eco destilado
agonía gozosa,
es tu poema del atrevido pulso
de río subterráneo...

Oigo tu voz, oculta no sé donde,
que desnuda se esparce
más viva cuando más impronunciada
y más cercana cuando más se esconde.

Epilogues for a Deceased Poet

Your departure convinces me you knew
you never walked alone
but behind the echo of your steps
other steps, echoless, followed you...

You knew the expected delight
of dying each day
and had the power to look at death
with your eyes closed.

Your plain, vibrating word
was sound and echo
as if already returning tired
from a faraway journey.

The life of your death was everything
anticipated and experienced
a conversation of blood and mystery
living within you.

The temperature of your words
—flame of ice,
living water burning cold—
penetrated your blood.

Your poetry cut like the edge
of a thin metal blade
not injuring the skin but within
on its cold contact.

Your poem—pure purity,
distilled echo, joyful agony—
is the bold flow
of a subterranean river...

I hear your hidden voice;
exposed, it scatters
—more alive when unspoken,
closer when hidden deeper.

69

Eres tan invisible que te veo
en lo más invisible,
en lo que por tan delgado y transparente
no se esconde el secreto.

Estoy cierto que vives difundido
en el cielo, en el aire,
en el agua, en el fuego
y también te descubro en el silencio
que conversa en el silencio mío.

Triángulo de silencios
1953

You are so invisible that I see you
in what is most invisible,
in what is so thin and transparent
even a secret cannot hide.

I am sure you live diffused
in sky, in air,
in water, in fire,
and I discover you in the silence
conversing with this silence of my own.

En cada mañana

En cada mañana, al despertar, resucitamos:
porque al dormir, morimos esas horas
en que libres del cuerpo, se recobra
la vida espiritual que antes tuvimos,
cuando aún no habitábamos la carne
que ahora nos define y nos limita,
y éramos, sin ser, misterio puro
en el ritmo total del universo.

Porque al dormir morimos sin saberlo;
nos vamos al espacio en ágil vuelo
sin perderla unidad que nos integra,
y somos como somos: idénticos, sin cambio,
extensos y desnudos
como el azul en el temblor del aire.
No extrañamos el cuerpo, no sufrimos
la ausencia de la piel que nos cobija;
somos como antes de nacer: etéreos,
vivos en plenitud de firmamento
y penetrantes como luz en sombras.

Y nadie, cuando duerme, acaso piense
que yace en los dominios de la muerte:
por que el cansancio, apenas agonía,
nos borra la razón,
desciende con ternura nuestros párpados,
apaga nuestros ojos,
anestesia la carne, y nos separa de ella
para robarnos vivos en el sueño.

Y esta costumbre de morir a diario,
sin dolor, sin sorpresa,
natural como el agua
que se deja atraer por el declive;
no nos deja pensar que es una muerte

Every Morning

When we wake each morning we come to life
because we die those hours we sleep.
Free of our body, we recover
the spiritual life we had before
when we did not yet possess the body
which now defines and limits us
and we were, without being, pure mystery
in the total rhythm of the universe.

When we sleep, we die without knowing it;
we go into space on an agile flight
without losing the unity that holds us together
and we are as we are: identical, without change,
complete and naked
like the blue in a tremor of air.
We do not miss our body, we do not suffer
the absence of the skin which covers us;
we are as we were before birth: eternal,
alive with the fullness of heaven
and penetrating like light in shadow.

On waking, none of us thinks
that we were lying in the domain of death:
through exhaustion, hardly agony,
our reason is erased,
our eyelids tenderly lowered,
closing our eyes,
relaxing our body, we separate from it
to steal ourselves alive into dreams.

And this habit of dying daily
without pain or surprise,
as natural as water
when it flows down hill,
does not let us think that we are dead

cada vez que dormimos,
y que, de cada muerte transitoria,
aprende nuestro sér
la verdad de morir su muerte eterna.

Nocturna Suma
1955

each time we sleep,
but with each transitory death
our being learns
the truth of dying its eternal death.

Poema íntimo

Si solamente tengo palabras y palabras
para decir mi angustia, mi sed de eternidad,
y las palabras son espejos desolados
que sus aguas no pueden la imagen reflejar.

Si en mis entrañas siento el vivo calofrío
del misterio de Dios, que quisiera expresar,
pero al querer hacerlo me fallan las palabras
porque la idea no cabe y las hace estallar.

¿Con qué pintar la espera que nace de mi sangre,
la voz que me circula, mi lejano mirar,
si las palabras son instantes de agonía
que en ecos se transforman, y mueren al azar?

¿Con qué cantar la música de todo lo soñado,
lo que sin ojos veo en mi ausencia carnal,
si las palabras son corolas de vacío
que al caerles mis sueños, no los pueden guardar?

¿Con qué grabar la línea del cuerpo imaginado,
las heridas de aroma que me deja el amor,
si las palabras son cadáveres errantes
y es imposible darles un nuevo corazón?

Si pudiera — no quiero — desterrar de mí mismo
este afán indomable de querer explicar
los estremecimientos del infierno secreto,
que no cesa un instante de creer y durar...

Si pudiera — no quiero — asfixiar la locura
que vuela sin sosiego tratando de encontrar
el lenguaje preciso, capaz de dar idea
de lo que ante el misterio me atrevo a imaginar...

Más tengo por fuerza que sentir lo que siento,
que sufrirlo en silencio y al exterior callar.
Poeta sin palabras, ¡qué terrible tormento!,
mi voz impronunciada me tiene que matar.

Nocturna Suma
1955

76

Intimate Poem

If I only have words and more words
to express my anguish, my eternal thirst,
and the words are desolate mirrors,
waters that cannot reflect an image.

If my insides feel the living chill
of the mystery of God which I want to express
but the words fail me when I try
because the idea doesn't fit and then explodes.

How can I paint the hope born in my blood,
the voice that circulates, my faraway stare,
if the words are instances of agony
transformed into echoes that die unexpectedly?

How can I sing the music of my dreams,
what I see without eyes in my bodily absence,
if the words are empty flower petals
impossible to save as they fall from my dreams?

How can I engrave the line of the imagined body,
the aromatic wounds that love leaves me,
if the words are wandering cadavers
and it's impossible to give them a new heart?

If I could — I don't want to — banish from myself
this wild eagerness to want to explain
the trembling of the secret hell that doesn't cease
for a moment to believe and endure...

If I could — I don't want to — smother the madness
flying wildly trying to find
the exact words, capable of giving ideas
to what I dare to imagine before the mystery ...

I would rather force myself to feel what I feel
than suffer in silence and appear to be calm.
A poet without words. What a terrible torment!
My unexpressed voice has to kill me.

Si hubieras sido tú

Si hubieras sido tú, lo que en las sombras, anoche,
bajó por la escalera del silencio
y se posó a mi lado,
para crear el cauce de acentos en vacío
que, me imagino, será el lenguaje de los muertos.
Si hubieras sido tú, de verdad, la nube sola
que detuvo su viaje debajo de mis párpados
y se adentró en mi sangre,
amoldándose a mi dolor reciente
de una manera leve, brisa, aroma,
casi contacto angelical soñado...
Si hubieras sido tú,
lo que apartando la quietud oscura
se apareció, tal como si fuera tu dibujo
espiritual, que ansiaba convencerme
de que sigues, sin cuerpo, viviendo en la otra vida.
Si hubieras sido tú la voz callada
que se infiltró en la voz de me conciencia,
buscado incorporarte en la palabra
que tu muerte expresaba con mis labios.
Si hubieras sido tú, lo que al dormirme
descendió como bruma, poco a poco,
y me fue encarcelando
en una vaga túnica de vuelo fallecido...

Si hubieras sido tú la llama llama
que inquemante creó, sin despertarme
ni conmover el lago del azoro:
tu inmaterial presencia,
igual que en el espejo emerge
la imagen, sin herirle
el límpido frescor de su epidermis.
Si hubieras sido tú...

If It Was You

If it was you who descended the stairway of silence
in the shadows last night
and rested beside me
to create the channel of voices from the void
which, I imagine, must be the language of the dead.
If it was you, truthfully, the single cloud
that paused its voyage beneath my eyelids
and entered my blood,
molding itself to my recent pain
lightly, like a breeze, fragrant,
almost the sound of angelic contact...
If it was you
who, parting the dark quiet,
appeared as if you were a spiritual image
anxious to convince me
that you go on, formless, living another life.
If it was you, the silent voice
that infiltrated the voice of my consciousness
looking to give shape in words
to what your death expressed from my lips.
If it was you who, when I fell asleep,
little by little, descended like mist,
and imprisoned me
in a hazy shroud of deceased flight...

If you were the flame that was created
without burning, calling me without waking
nor stirring the lake of restlessness,
your intangible presence,
like that of a mirror from which
the image emerges without injuring
the clean, refreshing air of its skin.
If it was you...

Pero nuestros sentidos corporales
no pueden identificar las ánimas.
Los muertos, si es que vuelven,
tal vez ya no conserven
los peculiares rasgos
que nos pudieran dar
la inmensa dicha de reconocerlos.
platicaba del amoroso asedio
con que la muerte sigue a nuestra vida.
Y hablábamos los dos adivinando,
haciendo conjeturas,
ajustando preguntas, inventando respuestas,
para quedar al fin
sumidos en derrota,
muriendo en vida por pensar la muerte.
Ahora tú ya sabes descifrar el misterio
porque estás en su seno, pero yo...

¿Quién más pudo venir a visitarme?
Recuerdo que, contigo solamente,
en esta incertidumbre secretamente pienso
que si no fuiste tú, lo que en las sombras, anoche,
bajó por la escalera del silencio
y se posó a mi lado,
entonces quizá fue
una vista de mi propia muerte.

Nocturna Suma
1955

But our bodily senses
cannot identify souls.
If they do return, perhaps
the dead no longer have
their unique features
which would give us
the good fortune of recognizing them.
Who else could have come to visit me?
I remember that I used to talk only
with you about the loving siege
that death wages against our life,
and the two of us would talk, guessing,
making conjectures
composing questions, inventing answers,
only to end up
completely defeated,
dying in life from thinking about death.
Now you already know how to unravel the mystery
because you are in its lap, but I...

In this uncertainty, I am secretly sure,
if it wasn't you who descended the stairway of silence
in the shadows last night,
and rested beside me,
then perhaps it was
a visit from my very own death.

Poema en las sombras

Los dos como sonámbulos buscando en las sombras
el pulso de una estrella nacida de nosotros,
que juntos, con el goce, gozando asesinamos.
A oscuras, tropezando, tocamos lo invisible
que las tinieblas forman con sus muros de asedio,
y tan sólo encontramos la soledad desnuda
exhalando en silencio sus latidos vacíos.

Ya nada existe ahora y los dos ambulamos
por caminos distintos y dolores iguales,
buscando sin sosiego la vida luminosa
de la frágil estrella que los dos apagamos.

Un día, sin esfuerzo, los dos nos cansaremos
de andar solos a solas por esta noche eterna,
y solos rodaremos a nuestras muertes solas;
pero entonces las muertes, con una nueva vida,
salvarán de las sombras la estrella que perdimos,
y en su luz ya seremos amor indivisible.

Nocturna Suma
1955

Poem in the Shadows

The two of us, like sleepwalkers in the shadows
looking for the pulse of a star born between us,
which we pleasantly to murdered.
Tripping in the dark, we found that invisible space
darkness forms with its wall of siege,
and we found naked solitude all alone
exhaling its empty beatings in silence.

Nothing exists now and the two walkers,
by different but painfully similar roads,
frantically look for the luminous life
of the fragile star they both put out.

One day, we will each tire
of walking alone, lonely, through this eternal night
and surround ourselves with our own lonely deaths;
but then our deaths, with a new life,
will save the star we lost from the shadows,
and in its light we will already be invisible love.

Nocturna suma

Deletreo el espacio y no comprendo
esas gotas de luz en plena noche,
que tiemblan, que se ensanchan, que se encogen,
y expresan desde el cielo
las frases de su pulso luminoso.

Yo no sé si es altura o es abismo
el sitio en donde asoman,
o si son o no son; pero las miro
como enjambre de islas en incendio
y sufro su atracción, su intento brillo,
su tímido mirar...

Las cuento, muchas veces, muchas veces...
Me olvido de la cuenta y me detengo
para empezar la cuenta nuevamente,
y la vuelvo a perder, cayendo siempre
en la fuga de un número disperso.
Y si gozo al contar, es porque siento
que busco a Dios, contando sus estrellas.

Nocturna suma
1955

84

Nocturne: *Summa*

I spell the heavens
but can't figure out those drops of light;
in the fullness of night they shimmer,
sparkle, and fade from the sky
expressing their luminous pulse.

That place where they appear —
I don't know if it's above or below —
or whether they exist or not, but I watch them
like clusters of islands on fire
and I give in to their attraction,
to their bright intensity and timid watching...

I have counted them many, many times...
I lose count and stop
to begin counting again
and again I lose count, always
in the flight of a falling star.
If I delight in counting, it's because
I am looking for God, counting his stars.

Nocturno cuerpo

Cuando de noche, a solas, en tinieblas,
fatigado de no sé qué fatiga
se derrumba mi cuerpo y se acomoda
a la impasible superficie oscura
que le sirve de apoyo y de mortaja,
yo me tiendo también y me limito
al inerme contorno que me entrega,
a la isla de olvido en que se olvida.

Separado de él y en él hundido
recuerdo que lo llevo todo el día
como cárcel de fiebre que me oprime,
como labios que dicen otras frases,
como instinto que burla mis deseos
o acciones desligadas de mi fuerza;
pero al mirarlo así, rendido fardo
indiferente en su actitud de piedra,
tigre de bronce, charco de silencio,
columna de cinismo derribada,
ciega figura en su lección de muerte:
yo lo percibo como carne intrusa,
como dolencia de una llaga ajena,
cómplice de un destino que no entiendo,
mudez que no lesiona mi palabra,
verdugo en anestesia secuestrado.

Y por eso al sentirme divido
y a la vez por su molde aprisionado,
analizo, sospecho, reflexiono
que sus muros endebles que me cercan
son fuego en orfandad, tierra robada,
agua sujeta en venas sumergidas
y aire sin aire arrebatado al aire;
que soy un prisionero de elementos
en honda combustión, que están buscando
fundir los eslabones que los unen

Nocturne: Body

Alone in the shadows of night,
tired by a tiredness I don't know,
my body collapses and gives in
to the dark, impassive surface
that serves as support and shroud.
I stretch out and also limit myself
to the defenseless contour that delivers me
to the island of oblivion where I forget.

Separated from him and submerged in him
I remember what I have carried around all day
like a jail of fever that oppresses me,
like lips that speak someone else's sentences,
like instinct that mocks my desires
or actions out of my control;
but seeing him like that, a bundle rendered
indifferent in his stone-like attitude
bronze tiger, silent pool,
fallen column of cynicism,
blind figure in its lesson of death;
I perceive him as intrusive flesh
like the ache of someone else's pain,
accomplice on a destiny I don't understand,
muteness that does not harm my word,
executioner in kidnapped anesthesia.

And so I feel myself divided
and at the same time imprisoned by a mold.
I analyze, suspect, and reflect
that its weak walls surrounding me
are fire in orphanhood, robbed earth,
water subjected in submerged veins
and air without air snatched from the air;
I am a prisoner of elements
in deep combustion, looking
to melt the links that unite them

para volver a la pureza intacta
el sitio universal donde eran libres:
la tierra pide su reposo en tierra,
el aire, su acrobacia transparente;
el fuego, la delicia de su llama;
y el agua: la blancura de su hielo,
su cause, o el prodigio de ser nube.
Al lado de él, lado y enraizado,
lo toco, lo examino desde adentro:
interior de una iglesia ensangrentada,
góticos arcos, junglas musculares,
entretejida pulsación de yedras,
laberinto de lumbre de amapolas
y entraña de una cripta en que se esconde
el numérico albor del esqueleto.

Y yo en medio de juez y de culpable,
de rebelde invasor y de invadido,
de mirar que descubre y se descubre,
de unidad que contempla sus facciones,
de pregunta privada de respuesta,
de espectador que sufre en propia carne
el corporal desgaste de que brotan
sus crecientes acopios de agonía.

Si soy su dueño ¿por qué lo palpo extraño,
despegado de mí— sombra de un árol —,
corteza sofocante de mi angustia,
vendaje que me oculta, ademe frágil,
imán que me atesora y me difunde,
materia que yo arrastro y que me arrastra?
Y estoy en él, presente, inevitable,
unido en el monólogo y la espera,
crecido en su reverso, y denunciado
por sus manos, sus ojos, sus pasiones,
la quemante ansiedad de sus delirios,
las brumas de sus tiempos que zozobra
y los relámpagos de su alegría.

to return to their intact purity,
to the universal site where they were free:
earth asks for its repose on earth,
air, its transparent acrobatics;
fire, the delight of its flame;
and water, the whiteness of ice,
its source, or the marvel of being cloud.
Beside him, sideways and rooted,
I touch him, examine him from within:
the interior of a bloody church,
Gothic arches, muscular jungles,
intertwined beating of ivy,
labyrinth of fire of poppies
and entrails of a crypt which hides
the numerical whiteness of the skeleton.

And I as judge and culprit,
of rebel invader and the invaded,
of watching what is discovered and discovering,
the whole which contemplates its parts,
the question deprived of answer,
the spectator that suffers the weakening
this growing excess of agony
causes in his own flesh.

If I am his owner, why do I feel estranged from him
disconnected from myself— shade of a tree —
suffocating bark of my anguish,
bandage that blindfolds me, fragile scaffold,
magnet keeping me together and pulling me apart,
matter that I drag and that drags me?
And I am in him, present and inevitable,
united in the monologue and the wait
growing behind his back, and betrayed
by his hands, his eyes, his passion,
the burning anxiety of his desires,
the mists of his times of floundering
and the lightning of his joy.

De adentro a fuera, de raíz a ramas,
presiono, me sublevo, abro mis fuerzas
para cavar, para acabar los muros
que viven de tenerme prisionero
pero un amor me nace y me detiene,
un fanatismo de vital amparo,
el apego del ánima y las células,
la intimidad de forma y contenido
acoplando sus ciegas superficies;
y me quedo conforme, sosegado
a la ajustada cárcel que me cubre
para seguir formando el nudo en fiebre
por el que siento que en verdad existo.

Agua, tierra, fuego y aire, en continua
aspersión de sus químicos halagos,
en escondida trabazón de empujes,
mandando y succionando sus mareas,
haciendo y deshaciendo lo que inician,
comiéndose a sí mismos, recreando
el desnudo valor de su estructura
en pugnas, atracciones y repechos,
porque quieren, anhelan, buscan, labran
la persistente acción que les devuelva
el vuelo original que poseían.

Esta unión de elementos, este nido
de físicas batallas, de incesantes
reacciones, es mi solo respaldo,
el trágico venero de la fuerza
que me sostiene aún hablando a solas.

Nocturna palabra
1960

From inside out, from root to branch,
I press, I revolt, I summon my strength
to dig, to finish the walls
that live to keep me prisoner
but love gives birth and holds me back,
a fanaticism of vital protection,
attachment of soul and cells,
connection of form and content
joining their blind surfaces;
and I remain calm, compliant
in the snug jail that covers me,
continuing to form the knot of fever
by which I feel that I truly exist.

Water, earth, fire, air in a continuous
sprinkling of their chemical flattery,
in hidden bond of pushing,
their tides ebbing and flowing,
doing and undoing what they initiate,
consuming themselves, recreating
the naked valor of their structure
in struggles, attractions and regressions
because they want, desire, seek, work toward
that persistent action which will return them to
the original flight they possessed.

This union of elements, this nest
of physical battles, of incessant
reactions, is my only support,
the tragic origin of the force
that sustains me even speaking all alone.

Nocturna palabra

Todo grito que hiere la delgadez del aire,
toda queja que alarga su dolorosa espina,
lo que se dice junto al cuerpo amado,
las plegarias volcadas
al pie de los altares de la duda,
la confusión babélica
en bullicio de lenguas espectrales,
el primer balbuceo
que al virgen labio despertó el azoro,
el canto eternizado
en la madurez que anhela repetirlo,
el alba de alegrías
o el son de las exequias:
subsisten en la atmósfera, insepultos,
desollados de sílabas,
en mimetismo con el vaho del mundo,
y libres en su ritmo giratorio
de concéntricas fugas sin naufragio.

Todo vive latente en el silencio
como en la sombra habita la luz muerta.
Por eso, algunas veces, en la noche,
cuando nada ni nada se denuncia
porque tierra, horizonte, luto y nubes
son una sola densidad sin labios:
del muro o la ventana,
del árbol o del viento,
asalta el bulto exacto de una frase,
la bruma corporal de algún pronombre,
o el súbito venero
de lumbre negra que agitada escribe
el hirsuto mensaje de sus llamas.

Yo miro, escucho, siento
ese desliz vacío, ese caer sin golpe,
esa atracción flotante

Nocturne: Word

Every cry injures the delicate air,
every complaint extends its painful thorn,
words spoken beside the beloved body,
the overturned petitions
at the feet of the altars of doubt,
the confusion of Babel
the bustle of spectral tongues
the first babbling
the virgin lip awakened,
the eternal chant
in the maturity that longs to repeat it,
the dawn of joys
or the sound of the requiem;
flayed syllables
subsist in the atmosphere, unburied,
mimic the breath of the world,
free of the revolving rhythm
of flying in circles without crashing.

Everything lives latent in silence
like the light of death inhabiting the shadow.
Sometimes at night then,
when nothing is spoken
earth, horizon, mourning and clouds
form a single voiceless unity:
from the wall or the window,
from the willow or the wind,
it assaults the shape of a phrase,
the corporal mist of some pronoun
or the sudden source
of black fire that writes
the rough message of its writhing flames.

I watch, listen, feel
that empty slip, that falling without a crash,
that floating attraction

93

que al estrechar el humo de sus tactos
pronuncia la mudez desesperada
del sumergido aliento del idioma.

Inaudible latir de excavaciones
son las palabras idas
que siguen existiendo, sin semblante,
en el libre escondite del espacio.
Son ánimas en pena
que imploran el instante que articule
el vértigo sonoro de su verbo,
o la mirada ardiente de unos ojos
que, al leerlas en su fosa de letras,
exhumen su vivencia
y de nuevo les hundan
el albor remozado de la imagen.

Una selva de voces sin sonido
oscila en la negrura
— perfumes sin corola, alas sin ángel
o pasiones cortadas de su fiebre —
anhelado encontrar
la boca que dé vida a las luciérnagas
de cada letra y amorosa entone
el virginal secreto que atesoran.

Cuando pongo el oído en el silencio
que la oscura quietud exalta y ciñe.
descubro en su mutismo
un habitar de roces,
un desdecir de acentos,
un tañido profundo del vacío
que, al penetrar la red de mis sentidos,
levanta por debajo de mi frente
la enardecida torre del monólogo.

Nocturna palabra
1960

which, pronounces the desperate silence
of the submerged breath of language
on embracing the smoke of its touch,

The spent words are the
inaudible beat of excavations
existing without recognition
in the free hiding place of space.
They are souls in grief
imploring the instant that articulates
the sonorous vertigo of their verb,
or the ardent look of some eyes
reading them in their grave of letters,
exhuming their experience
only to sink again
to the renewed dawn of the image.

A forest of soundless voices
oscillates in the blackness
— aroma without flower, wings without angel
or passions cut from their heat —
longing to find the mouth
that gives life to the fireflies
of each letter and longingly intones
the original secret they hold.

When I put my ear to the silence
the dark quiet exhales and binds,
I discover in its muteness
a dwelling of friction,
a contradiction of accents,
a profound tolling of the void
penetrating the network of my senses,
raising from beneath my face
the inflamed tower of the monologue.

Nocturno amor
(Fragmento)

V.

Naciste a mis entrañas vinculado
en creciente raíz, cósmico nudo;
de mi selva interior el potro rudo
que anhela libertad, enamorado.

Soy mortaja y estoy, amor, tajado
por tu evasión continua que no eludo
sino que vuelo en ti, y aquí me escudo,
para que al volver seas amparado.

Venero de tus ímpetus me ligo
a tu fuga celeste, a tu caída,
a la expansión total de tus secretos;

pero de noche, cuando estoy contigo,
recobro con tu fuerza sumergida
la sola soledad de estar completo.

Nocturna palabra
1960

Nocturne: Love
(Fragment)

5.

You were born in me, entwined
in a growing root, a cosmic knot;
deep within me, the rambunctious colt
longs for freedom, in love.

I am shroud and I am wounded, love,
by your continuous evasion which I do not elude
but I fly to you and arm myself
to protect you when you return.

Source of your impetus, I commit myself
to your celestial fleeing, to your fall,
to the total expansiveness of your secrets;

but at night, when I am with you,
with your submerged strength I recover
the loneliness of being complete.

Nocturno en llamas

I

Antes de haber nacido, cuando apenas
en las galaxias era calofrío,
o la sed en rotación por el vacío,
o sangre sin la cárcel de las venas;

antes de ser en túnica de arenas
un angustiado palpitar sombrío,
antes, mucho antes que este cuerpo mío
supiera de esperanzas y de penas:

ya buscaba tu nombre, tu semblante,
el disperso latir de tu vivencia,
tu mirada en las nubes esparcida;

porque, desde el asomo delirante
de mis instintos ciegos, tu existencia
era ya por mis ansias presentida.

II

¿Quién puedo acudir en mi tortura?
¿A qué divinidad, a qué lucero
podré rogar que lleve a lo que quiero
este amargo sabor de mi dulzura?

¿A quién debo llamar en esta oscura
quemazón de mi sangre en que yo muero?
¿A quién, en el dolor que desespero,
podré implorar un poco de ternura?

¿A quién, a quién en mi amoroso infierno
confesaré la exacta biografía
de me secreto amor enardecido?

Debe de hacer en el girar eterno
algo, que al escuchar mi voz sombría
le lleve mis palabras a su oído.

98

Nocturne: In Flames

I

Before I was born, when
the galaxies were scarcely a shiver
or a thirst in rotation through emptiness,
or blood without the prison of veins;

before being an anguished shadow
pulsing in a tunic of sand,
long, long before this body of mine
knew hope and sorrow:

I looked for your name, your likeness,
the stray beating of your experience,
your glance in the scattered clouds;

because, before the delirious appearance
of my blind instincts, longingly
I already sensed your existence.

II

Who can I turn to in my torture?
What divinity, which bright star
can I ask to give this bitter
sweetness to someone else?

Who should I call in this dark,
burning blood where I am dying?
Who can I beg for a bit of tenderness
in this pain of despair?

Who in my loving hell will hear
the confession of my true life story
of my secret, inflamed love? Who?

In the great, eternal turning, I must do
something, so when he hears my voice
he will lift my words to his ear.

III

¿Cuántas transmutaciones has pasado?
¿Cuántos siglos de luz, cuántos colores,
nebulosas, crepúsculos y flores
para llegar a ser, has transitado?

¿En qué constelaciones has brillado?
Después de cuántas muertes y dolores,
de huracanes, relámpagos y albores
la forma corporal has conquistado?

No puede concebir mi pensamiento
esa edad atmosférica que hicimos
en giratorio espera; mas yo siento

que milenios de lumbres anduvimos
esperanzados en el firmamento,
hasta unir este amor con que existimos.

IV

Cuando tus ojos abren la mirada,
se asoman los vestigios verdaderos
que donaron la vida a los luceros
y pasión a la tierra inanimada.

En tu existencia veo, transparentada,
la historia virginal de los primeros
espasmos de la luz, y los veneros
de la girante red astralizada.

Al estrechar tu cuerpo, siento mío
el Universo todo, y las vertientes
de sus cósmicas leyes que nos rigen,

porque tu lumbre llena de vacío
y, al fundirnos, se engranan los ardientes
imanes de la fuerza del origen.

III

How many transmutations have you endured?
Through how many centuries of light, colors,
nebulas, twilights and flowers
yet to be, have you journeyed?

In which constellations have you sparkled?
How much sorrow, how many deaths,
hurricanes, lightning bolts and dawns
before you achieved bodily form?

My thoughts cannot conceive
of that atmospheric age we spent
in revolving wait; but I feel

that we traveled millennia of light
waiting in the firmament,
to be united now in this existence of love.

IV

When your eyes opened
to the view, you saw what truly
gave life to the brightest stars
and passion to the lifeless earth.

In your existence I clearly see
the opening history of the first
spasms of light and the source
of the spinning network of stars.

Embracing your body, my own
feels the entire universe, and the rules
of its cosmic laws that govern us,

because your light fills the emptiness
and when we melt together, the burning
attraction of the forces of origin fuse.

101

V

En esta soledad de sombra pura,
de quietud en constante movimiento,
de mudez que enardece el pensamiento
en lucha negra con la noche oscura:

cabe todo el raudal de la amargura,
el río del moral presentimiento,
la cóncava atracción del firmamento,
y el amor, al amor que me tortura.

En este pulso de tiniebla viva
en que el insomnio su vigor levanta
buscando conectar mis ansiedades,

puedo yo, con la ráfaga instintiva
del anhelo de amar que se agiganta,
vivir en un instante, eternidades.

Nocturna palabra
1960

V

In this solitude of pure shadow,
of quietness in constant movement,
of muteness that burns thought
in the black struggle of the dark night:

all the torrents of bitterness fit,
the river of moral premonitions,
the concave attraction of the firmament
and love, the love that tortures me.

In this pulse of living darkness
where insomnia gathers its strength
trying to connect my yearnings,

with the natural desire
to love growing beyond bounds,
I can live eternities in an instant.

Inmortalidad del Comandante Guevara

Asesinaron tu cuerpo, CHE GUEVARA,
pero no tu presencia: en las selvas
sigues cabalgando.
Escondieron tu cuerpo, CHE GUEVARA,
pero sigues viviendo
en el pulso indetenible de las horas,
te sentimos disfrazado
de montaña, de relámpago,
de mar embravecido,
de árbol milenario
o de inmenso paisaje libertario.

Apagaron tu palabra, CHE GUEVARA,
pero sigues hablando
en el temblor del aire,
en el río labriego, en la mañana campesina
y en los cañaverales
que practican
su constante ejercicio militar.

Amputaron tus manos, CHE GUEVARA,
pero las sigues moviendo
en el calosfrío de los follajes,
en el aplauso de las palmeras,
en la marea de los trigales,
en el aleteo de las palomas
y en las manos nuevas
del valiente rebelde americano.

Robaron tus ojos, CHE GUEVARA,
pero nos sigues viendo
con la limpia mirada de los niños,
en el Sol que despierta cada día,
con el alto latir de las estrellas
y con los bosques color de la esperanza.
Estás en los elementos

The Immortality of Commandant Guevara

They murdered your body, CHE GUEVARA,
but not your presence: you keep on
riding in the jungles.
They hid your body, CHE GUEVARA,
but you keep on living
in the unstoppable pulse of hours,
we feel you disguised
as mountain, as lightning,
as the angry sea,
the millennial tree
or the vast, free countryside.

They extinguished your word, CHE GUEVARA,
but you keep on speaking
in the tremor of air,
in the working river, in the country morning
and in the sugarcane fields
that practice
their constant military exercise.

They cut off your hands, CHE GUEVARA,
but you keep moving them
in the shimmering foliage,
in the applause of the palm trees,
in the waving fields of wheat,
in the fluttering of the doves
and in the new hands
of the brave American rebel.

They stole your eyes, CHE GUEVARA,
but you keep watching us
with the fresh look of children,
in the sun that rises each day,
with the lofty beating of the stars
and with the forests colored by hope.
You are in the elements

y en la germinación constante
de todas las semillas.
Cantas en el ave,
en el corazón de fuego,
en las heladas brasas de la nieve,
en la ira del agua
y en el cambiante color de los horizontes.

COMANDANTE GUEVARA:
desde la ubicuidad de tu reino
ayuda al gran pueblo Vietnamita
para *que les dé en toda la madre*
a los perversos invasores;
enseña a los negros
para que exterminen la crueldad
de los blancos;
injerta pólvora en el corazón
del coreano
para que luche y recobre
la unidad de su patria;
y tu América, CHE GUEVARA, tu América
explotada, invadida, discriminada,
espera tu reencarnación
en cada hombre digno de ser hombre.

¡CHE GUEVARA, moderno CRISTO GUERRILLERO!
desde tu muerte
tu América se siente menos sola
porque vives fundido
en la creciente luz de su esperanza.

1968

and in the constant germination
of all seeds.
You sing with the bird
in the heart of the fire,
in the frozen embers of snow,
in the rage of the water
and in the changing color of the horizons.

COMMANDANT GUEVARA:
from your omnipresent kingdom
you help the great Vietnamese people
so *that they can screw*
their evil invaders;
you teach the Blacks
how to end the cruelty
of the Whites;
you inject gunpowder into the hearts
of the Koreans
so that they fight to recover
the unity of their country:
and your America, CHE GUEVARA, your America
exploited, invaded, discriminated,
awaits your reincarnation
in every man worthy of being a man.

CHE GUVERARA, modern WARRIOR CHRIST!
since your death
your America feels less lonely
because you live fused
in the growing light of its hope.

Nocturno Ciego

Testamento para el hombre universal
...y el hombre creó a Dios
a su imagen y semejanza.
DIOS
es
la suprema ausencia.
La suprema ausencia
es DIOS
(Lo sabemos
mi soledad y yo).

Pensar en Dios, querer desentrañarlo;
abrir el aire y percibir el pulso
del invisible arropo de su fuerza;
buscarlo con los ojos de la duda,
asirlo de la cuenca de vacío
y reducir su inmensidad creciente
a una presencia de unidad palpable.

Gozar de fe, con místico arrebato,
para seguir con ansiedad creyente
los rasgos gigantescos de su rostro
hasta perdernos en alturas hondas;
después de rodar por variedad de abismos
con el hueco preciso de un volumen
que al estrecharlo se deshiela en humo.

Levantarnos henchidos de soberbia
y subir — en derrame imaginario
que aniquila plegarias y destruye
el bíblico calor que nos alienta —,
hasta el tiempo sin ojos del vacío,
hasta el clima difunto del espacio
y desde allá caer desvanecidos
en la isla más sola de la angustia.

Hundirnos en la noche concentrada
que el espesor de nuestra carne esconde

Nocturne: Blind

Testament for the universal man
...and man created God
in his image and likeness.
God:
the supreme absence.
Supreme absence:
God.

(This we know,
my solitude and I).

To think about God: to long to decipher him —
to split the air and feel the pulse
of the invisible cloak of his force;
to look for him with doubtful eyes,
to seize him from the hollow of nothingness
and to shrink his vast increase
to a single here and now.

To savor faith with mystic rapture
and to trace his monumental face
with faithful longing
losing ourselves in the highest depths;
after tumbling through many an abyss
with the crisp hollow of great volume
that melts in smoke when touched.

Swollen with arrogance, we arise
and climb — on the imaginary outpouring
that wipes out prayers and destroys
the biblical warmth that gives us breath —
to the eyeless time of the emptiness
to the dead weakness of the stars
and from there to fall, banished,
to the loneliest island of anguish.

To sink in the dense night
which the bulk of our flesh hides

como en la arena de la playa lo hace
el cangrejo medroso. Ya en el fondo
de le negrura de la propia entraña,
disecar sin descanso sus tinieblas
y proseguir hurgan do por los huesos,
por el llanto, las olas y las venas
hasta alcanzar la cruz de la derrota
y el naufragio del cuerpo en la conciencia

Rehacernos, gritar, reconfortarnos,
resurgir de las sombras con más furia
a desgajar el íntimo fracaso
y volver a los mismo, sin demora,
continuando la búsqueda, el rastreo,
la bajada tenaz dentro del tórax
y el salto sin avance hacia la altura.
En la lucha sentirnos arrojados
a la tortura de las reflexiones,
a volar y volver al mismo nudo,
a girar y girar en pensamiento
por la espalda del cielo, por las cumbres,
por el encono de los vendavales
o el nevado silencio de los astros.

Pensar en Dios, querer estructurarlo
agrupando diversas fantasías
que, al ensamblar sus nítidos contrastes,
estallan en escombros que se pierden
en caída mortal hacia las nubes,
para dejarnos truncos, convencidos
de que se vuelve mucho más inmenso
cuanto con más vigor lo imaginamos.

Pensarlo y escuchar el abejeo
de los rezos lejanos del idólatra,
del monótono canto primitivo
adorando las gotas siderales,
de los ecos de antiguas religiones

like the timid crab in the sand
on the beach. Already in the black
depths of its own entrails,
ceaselessly dissecting its shadows,
it keeps on sifting through the bones,
through the wailing, the waves, the veins
until reaching the cross of defeat —
the collapse of the body within the conscience.

To pull ourselves together: to shriek,
to come back from the shadows with more fury
to destroy the intimate failure
and to return again to what we were before,
continuing the search, the tracking,
the stubborn descent within the chest
and the futile leap toward the heights.
In the battle, to feel ourselves hurled
into the torture of our contemplation,
to fly and to return to the same knot,
spinning and spinning in thought
over the back of the sky, over the summits
through the malice of wind storms
or the snow-covered silence of the stars.

To think about God: to want to create him
by gathering together diverse fantasies
highlighting their sharp contrasts,
that explode into debris and get lost
in the mortal fall toward the clouds
leaving us cut off, certain
that he becomes more immense
the harder we imagine him.

To think about him: to hear the buzz
of far-off idolatrous prayers,
the dull, repetitive chant
adoring the splashes of the stars,
the echoes of ancient religions

que musitan el pregón desesperado
de su abolida fe, de los intensos
golpes exactos de guerreras danzas
y todos los torrentes de invenciones
que el humano candor ha eslabonado
para esculpir los dioses, los demonios,
los ídolos en éxtasis agudo:
que por detrás del tiempo fenecido
aguardan el momento de filtrarse,
de renacer su afán indestructible
para juntarlo, y proseguir la fuerza
de la misma ansiedad que desde siempre
viene incendiando el corazón del hombre.

Mirarlo y contemplar el infinito
saliendo de sus ojos sin miradas:
fragua de estrellas, huracán de asombros,
almendra de la física, dinamo
que impulsa la locura giratoria,
amparo sin efigie, hondura huyente,
ira en acecho, manantial de rayos,
etéreo lanzador de los cometas,
furiosa tempestad que inspira el miedo,
verdugo que se esconde en el prodigio,
hacedor de la vida y de la muerte,
hambre perpetua del delirio cósmico
que asila y desvanece lo que crea,
abismo que se encara boca abajo
para echarnos encima los latidos
de sus distantes huecos luminosos.

Contemplarlo y mirar el firmamento
emergido del hueco de sus manos:
vía láctea colmada de jazmines,
pista de Venus, lago de la Luna,
muralla de constantes parpadeos,
regazo de palomas planetarias,

that murmur hopeless cries
of their abolished faith, of the intense,
measured beatings of war dances
and the torrent of inventions
that human naiveté has linked together
in order to sculpt gods and demons,
idols in acute ecstasy
lurking in times past,
waiting the chance to overtake us
and revive their endless urge,
to reunite and continue intensely,
the same yearning that
forever sets man's heart on fire.

To watch him: to contemplate the infinite
turning away of his unseeing eyes —
forge of stars, hurricane of amazement,
source of physics, dynamo
that propels the revolving insanity,
protection without effigy, fleeing depths,
fury in waiting, geyser of rays,
ethereal launcher of comets,
furious storm that inspires fear,
executioner who hides in his magic,
maker of life and death,
perpetual hunger of cosmic delirium
protecting and rejecting what he creates,
abyss that looks face-down
to drop us onto the beating
of its distant, luminous cavities.

To contemplate him: to look at the firmament
emerged from the hollow of his hands —
Milky Way filled with jasmines,
Trail of Venus, Lake of the Moon,
ceiling of constant twinkling
refuge of planetary doves,

ábaco en que intentamos hacer sumas
de las hondas distancias que nos sitian;
avicultura de las albas, fuente
que derrama las noches y los días.

Casi palparlo y descubrir la tierra
surgiendo de las olas de su sangre:
manzana sostenida en horizontes,
redondez con los rasgos de sus bosques,
superficie tatuada por los mares,
cumbres que embisten con pezón de albura,
laderas con rebaños de esmeraldas
y las nubes saliendo de los lagos
recién desnudas, en pureza libre,
para subir a enflorecer el cielo.

Pensar en Dios, pensar y confundirlo
con el sol, con la estrella, con la Luna,
con los milagros físicos del agua,
con el tacto flotante de la brisa,
con el astro terreno de la rosa,
con la entraña vital de la semilla
y con la atmósfera que nos rodea;
porque todos los seres y las cosas
denuncian, a través de su estructura,
el secreto interior que nos genera,
el nervio de recóndita energía,
que les impone forma, vientre, pulso
y los hace ocupar dentro del orbe
el sitio exacto donde desenvuelven
amor, fecundidad, acción y muerte.
(Y nosotros — razón desorbitada
y a los cinco sentidos constreñida —
confundimos a Dios, con lo que engendra
la sola emanación de su misterio).

Meditarlo y sentir que lo formamos
con frondas de nostalgia, con suplicios

abacus on which we try to calculate
from the deep distances besieging us,
farming of dawns, fountain
that spills out the days and nights.

To almost touch him: to discover the earth
surging in the waves of his blood —
an orb held up by its horizons,
roundness with traces of its forests,
tattooed surface of the seas,
summits with white peaks that attack,
slopes with flocks of emeralds
and clouds forming from recently
stripped lakes, in pure abandonment,
to rise and fill the heaven with blossoms.

To think about God: to confuse him
with the sun, the stars, the moon,
with the physical miracles of water,
with the floating touch of a breeze,
with the earthly star of a rose.
with the life-giving core of a seed
and with the atmosphere that surrounds us;
because all beings and things
through their structure, betray
the inner secret that generates us,
that nerve of hidden energy
which gives them form, womb, pulse
and makes them occupy their exact space
within the orb where they unfold
love, fertility, action and death.
(And we — excessive reason
constrained by our five senses —
confuse God with the unique show
that his mystery begets).

To meditate: to feel that we form him
with nostalgic fronds, with the torture

de reflexión de desolada espera,
con múltiples espinas de temores,
con salino deslave de recuerdos,
con alargados pétalos de angustia
y con la ebullición de los monólogos.

Adivinarlo a oscuras, dilatados
en la terca evasión que nos ensancha,
y a la vez oprimidos por el cerco
del molde corporal que nos con tiene:
fogata que agiganta su tamaño
con el humo viajero que despide...

Decididos, donarle semejanza
para poder atesorar su forma,
seguir el litoral de su tiniebla,
darle línea al vislumbre de su amparo,
incensar su vacío y dar de golpes
en el aire, en la luz, en el silencio,
y sufrir la tragedia indefinible
del peso universal sobre la frente.

Abolirlo y sentir que se nos cae
toda la eternidad de soledades
para hacernos sentir que nadie capta
nuestro crecido embate de miradas,
y que todo el inmenso laberinto
alumbrado, nocturno, neblinoso
que envuelve a la medusa de los rumbos:
es espejismo sideral, sesteo
de luminosidades descarriadas,
fumarolas del cráter del vacío,
ánimas de milenios de luz rota
o polvo de los fósiles celestes.

Convencidos, negarlo con denuedo,
presentir su lejana cercanía,
adivinar su aliento en cada cosa,

of reflection in desperate wait,
with multiple thorns of fear,
with salty erosion of memories,
with extended petals of anguish
and with bubbling monologues.

To guess in the dark, waiting
in the stubborn evasion that opens us,
and at the same time oppressed
by the physical mold that contains us:
a bonfire that grows,
its drifting smoke floating away...

Determined, we make him like us
in order to hold onto his form,
following his coastline in the dimness,
giving shape to the glimpse of his protection,
flattering his emptiness and beating
the air, the light, the silence,
suffering the inexplicable tragedy
of the universal weight on our shoulders.

To abolish him: to sense
an eternity of solitude slipping away
making us feel that no one grasps
our growing onslaught of glances
and that the entire, immense,
misty, foggy labyrinth
that surrounds our tangled paths
is a stellar illusion. I rest
from the luminous false path,
the smoking hole of the crater of emptiness,
souls of millennia of broken light
or dust of celestial fossils.

Convinced, to deny him bravely,
to sense his close distance,
to guess his breath in each thing,

117

odiarlo como el ciego odia su noche
y lanzarle el insomnio interrogante
como zarpazo de dolor que busca
desencajar la voz, de su silencio.

Inquirentes caer en el espacio
con su veloz asenso — como piedras
que del suelo rodaran cuesta arriba
y el avance las fuera carcomiendo
adarme por adarme —, hasta que quedarnos
libres de todo peso y toda forma,
disgregados en nada y deglutidos
por la insaciable gula giratoria.

Salirnos del pavor... Revincularnos
juntando y rentando lo que fuimos
y volver a vivir el mismo cuerpo,
la misma pesadumbre, el mismo llanto,
el terco afán de asir, de lo inasible,
eso mismo inasible que nos hizo...

Convencernos por fin que solo somos
un arranque de huérfanos latidos:
la continuada sucesión de instantes
que llega apenas a la suma vega
de cuarenta millones de minutos,
que son el lapso que nos pertenece
para marcar la huella de unos pasos,
devolver la inocencia a unas palabras,
inventar la pasión de nuevos besos
y con la audacia de las conjeturas,
escorzar la silueta del origen.

Acabar por sabernos dueños solos
de la muerte que busca madurarse
en el árbol de sangre que ocultamos
y que, indefensos ante su embestida
que por fuera y por dentro nos impone:
sólo queda oponerle a su victoria

118

to hate him like the blind hates his night
and to throw our questioning insomnia
at him like a lash of pain that tries
to release its voice from silence.

Searchers falling through space —
our speeding ascent like stones
rolling up hill along the ground,
eroding away bit by bit
— until we are left free
of all weight and form,
disintegrated into nothingness
and swallowed by an insatiable greed.

To leave dread... To join together,
reconnecting to what we were and returning
to live in the same body, the same nightmare,
the same lament, the same stubbornness
to grasp, from what cannot be grasped,
the same untouchable source that created us...

To convince ourselves that we are finally
only an outburst of pulsing orphans:
a continuous succession of instants
that barely reaches a total of perhaps
some forty million minutes
— the time that belongs to each of us
to leave the footprint of a few steps,
to return innocence to some words,
to invent the passion of new kisses
and, with the audacity of guessing,
to bring depth to the outline of origin.

To end up knowing we are only owners
of a death that seeks to be matured
in the tree of blood we hide,
defenseless before the attack,
it imposes on us both inside and out:
the only thing to prevent its victory

119

el poema que nazca, al ser leído,
la penumbra de alguna profecía,
el trazo de un dolor en el tramonto,
las huellas digitales de los sueños
o el ánima de las palabras idas
que recobre la voz de otros labios.

Es natural morir. La muerte es nuestra
como es nuestra la angustia de estar solos
y el ansia de vivir que nos sustenta;
pero antes de caer, hay que ser fuertes
para grabar indicios en las rocas,
plantar el roble de afligidas ramas
como verde señal de nuestro viaje;
iniciar un desmonte de vereda
y, en el profundo caracol de sombras,
dejar latente el ambulante fluido
que, sin ser vistos, nuestra acción repita
cuando incorpóreos nos esconda el aire.

La trágica verdad hay que encararla
aunque implique admitir que sólo somos
unas horas de fuego en desatino
que, al consumirse, escasamente deja
un tímido desvelo de cenizas
que el viento, a tientas, lo levanta y lleva
hasta el encuentro con un lodo extraño,
Pero aunque presintamos el naufragio,
tenemos el deber de amar la vida
como si fuera eternidad palpable
y, olvidando el acecho permanente
del ángel espacial que nos inmola,
henchir impulsos que atrevidos luchen
por dejar un taladro en la negrura,
vivir la plenitud de flor abierta,
y aceptar el final irremediable
no como víctimas, sino como hombres.
¡Hay que morir, pero quedar despiertos!

is the poem born to be read,
the half-light of some prophecy,
the line of pain in the fierce north wind,
the fingerprints of dreams
or the spirit of departed words
that recovers their voice from another's lips.

It is natural to die: Death is ours
just as the anguish of being alone
and the longing to live that sustains us;
but before falling, we must be strong
in order to engrave traces on the rocks,
to plant the oak of afflicted branches
as green evidence of our passage;
to initiate a change of path
and to leave the flowing fluid dormant
in the spiral of deep shadows
without being seen, our action repeats,
when we are bodiless, hidden by air.

To face the tragic truth
although admitting it implies we are only
a few hours of foolish fire
that burns out
leaving a timid remnant of ashes
that the groping wind lifts and carries
until they drift someplace else.
Although we anticipate the shipwreck,
we have the obligation to love life
as if it were a palpable eternity
forgetting the perpetual spying
of the spatial angel that sacrifices us,
suppressing the impulses that dare fight,
by piercing the darkness,
to live the fullness of a flower in bloom
and to accept the unavoidable end
not as victims, but as men.
We must die, but stay awake!

Gritarle a Dios, sentir que no nos oye,
asumir la verdad de que es ausencia
y descubrirnos solos, desolados,
con una soledad desvinculada
que vagando en la noche sin orillas
anhela descubrir punto de apoyo...

Y, sin embargo, abrirnos en miradas
para ver el espacio, como nuestro;
la tierra, como sólida ternura
y, el universo entero, como único
nido sin muros que nos da refugio.

Gritarle a Dios, gritarle con denuedo,
increpar su mudez con desafío,
exigir que nos diga lo que somos,
a qué vinimos y por qué nos vamos...
Y al no tener respuesta ni mirada,
deducir que nosotros lo inventamos
con la espera, el pavor, la angustia en vilo,
y el anhelo de hacernos inmortales

Conscientes, convencidos, exaltados,
vivir la realidad, y con audacia
izar la percepción de los sentidos
y la imaginación en plena lumbre,
para formar lo eterno con lo efímero.
Al borde de las horas corredizas,
con urgente avidez ramificada
beber el alto brillo del lucero,
ascender por el canto de lo pájaros,
descifrar el mensaje de las nubes,
entender el silencio de la Luna
y tocar las distancias con los sueños,
(Juntando briznas de emoción se puede
dejar el pulso que nos sobreviva).

Buscar a Dios, pero buscarlo dentro
del colectivo mar de nuestra sangre

122

To wail at God: to feel he doesn't hear us,
to assume the truth of his absence
and to find ourselves alone, desolate,
with a disconnected loneliness
that wanders in the shoreless night,
longing to find some place of comfort...

Still, we turn our vision toward space
to make it like our own;
the earth, like solid tenderness
and the entire universe as a unique
nest without walls to protect us.

To laugh hysterically at God:
to challenge his silence with courage,
to demand that he tell us what we are,
why we are here and where we are going...
And with no response or even glance,
we conclude that we invented him
with hope, fear, expected longing
and a yearning to become immortal.

Conscious, convinced, exalted,
to really live, boldly hoisting
the perception of the senses
and the imagination in full light,
to merge the eternal with the ephemeral.
On the edge of fleeting hours,
with an urgent eagerness
to take in the brilliance of the bright star
to rise on the song of the birds,
to decipher the message of the clouds,
to understand the silence of the moon
and to touch the distances with dreams.
(Braiding strands of emotions, we can
leave behind a pulse that survives us).

To search for God: to look for him instead
in the collective sea of our blood

de donde nace, crece y se desborda
en amplitud de excavación aérea;
palpar su formación, su crecimiento,
su emanciparse de nosotros mismos
como propio torrente que nos alza
en circular escala de ascensiones.
Convencernos que nace de nosotros
como germinación indetenible
de nostalgia de origen, o de anhelo
sediento de su centro de energía.

Ya, por fin, advertir que lo creamos
por la necesidad inevitable
de no sentirnos solos, y el sonsuelo
de ganar un amparo que extermine
esta terca obsesión, este suplicio
de saber que seremos solo polvo,
polvo contrito, polvo sin memoria,
sufrido polvo en la orfandad del polvo...

Liberados, sin falsas esperanzas,
únicos dueños de nuestro albedrío
y sin miedo a venganzas o castigos:
gozar naturalmente la existencia
estrenando la vida cada día
con un creciente amor y, enamorados
de cielo y astros, mares y horizontes,
nubes y rosas, árboles y frutos,
escanciar el deleite, y completarnos
para nunca sentir que somos huérfanos,
solos y esclavos de un destino mudo...

Sin esperar el cielo prometido
ni temer un infierno incinerante,
ni juez que nos perdone o nos condene
al juzgar nuestros actos, o verdugo
que se goce de vernos en las llamas:
estar conformes con vivir el tiempo

where he is born, grows, and overflows
in the fullness of space.
To feel his formation, his growth,
his freeing himself from us
like a torrent that lifts us
in a rising circular scale.
To convince ourselves that he is born of us
like an unstoppable germination
of nostalgia of origin, or a longing
thirst from the center of energy.

Finally, to realize that we create him
because of our inevitable need
not to feel alone, and the consolation
of gaining refuge that eliminates
this stubborn obsession, this torture
of knowing that we will be only dust
contrite dust, dust without memory,
long-suffering orphans of dust...

Freed at last, without false hopes,
owners of our own will
without fear of revenge or punishment:
to enjoy the natural existence
that life gives us each day
with increasing love and, in love with
the sky, planets, seas and horizons,
clouds, roses, trees and their fruits,
to share the delight that completes us,
never again to feel that we are lonely
orphans or slaves of our silent destiny...

Without waiting for the promised heaven
or the fear of a burning hell
or a judge who will pardon or condemn
when weighing our actions, or executioner
who enjoys seeing us in flames:
we agree to live in the time

que el azar nos depare, resignados
a la dicha, al martirio, o la alegría
y, en nudo ciego, el cuerpo y la conciencia,
que afronten los dolores y la dicha
con valor, gota a gota saboreados,
sabiéndonos, amorosos, nuestra vida
y aceptar, sin recelos, nuestra muerte.
Si asomara el desquicio, o presintamos
el delirante espiritual derrumbe:
exacerbar la íntima certeza
de que alguna razón tuvo el misterio,
el orbe insomne, la energía suprema
o la pasión del universo en llamas;
para crear sobre la tierra, el hombre.

Como vuelven las aguas de los ríos
al seno de los mares, y les llevan
en cada gota la experiencia exacta
de su largo correr; tal vez nosotros,
al ser la desnudez de la sustancia
que se reinstala en el secreto ritmo
de la eterna creación, podamos darle
la completa experiencia de una vida
vivida, conmovida, electrizada
que, al consumar su tránsito terrestre,
hizo el acendramiento de su fuerza
para crecerla y ascender de nuevo
al cumplimiento de su astral oficio.

Nocturna Palabra
1960–1988

Este poema se ha vuelto mi obsesión diletante. En la primera edición, México, FCE, 1960, apareció como lo concebí. En la segunda edición de la UNAM, le hice algunos cambios y, en esta edición de Domés, lo podé cuanto era posible. Ya es el último intento que puedo hacer buscando su esclarecimiento y perfección. Ojalá y haya un poeta que lo apasione y quiera ayudarme a terminarlo. Desde mi ausencia definitiva se lo agradeceré.

that chance offers us, resigned
to happiness, martyrdom, or joy and,
in blind union, to the body and conscience,
that confront pain and happiness
bravely, enjoying each drop,
lovingly knowing our life
and accepting our death without suspicion.
If this appears as madness, or if we anticipate
the delirious spiritual collapse:
to challenge the intimate certainty
that the mystery held for some reason,
the sleepless orb, the supreme energy
or the passion of the universe in flames
in order to create man on earth.

As the waters of the river
return to the bosom of the sea,
each drop carrying the singular experience
of its long flow, perhaps we,
being the simplest essence of the substance
that returns in the secret rhythm
of eternal creation, may give him
the full experience of a life
lived, touched, energized, one that,
has completed the purification of itself
and grown and ascended once again
to the fulfillment of its astral duty.
on completing its earthly journey.

This poem has turned into my dilettantish obsession. In the first edition, Mexico, FCE (Fondo de Cultura Económica), 1960, it appeared as I conceived it. In the second edition by UNAM (Universidad Nacional Autónoma de México), I made some changes and in this edition by Donés, I've done as much as I could. This is the last effort I can make trying to clarify and perfect it. I hope some poet will become passionate about it and want to help me finish it. From my definitive silence, I will be grateful.

Nocturno alquimia de mis sueños

Yo te amo como se ama a una estrella:
puedo atreverme a contemplar tu albor,
a sentir tu pureza luminosa,
a escalar con mis ansias
la altura en que te asomas;
pero nunca a tocarte
ni a sembrar mi caricias
en la fulgente piel de tu misterio.

Yo sé dónde apareces diariamente,
conozco el sitio exacto
y la hora precisa
en que tu rostro enciende su hermosura.
Aprendí de memoria
tu órbita celeste,
el instante glorioso
en que brillas más cerca de mis ojos
y también el momento
en que huyendo me robas tu semblante.

Yo sé que soy tu dueño distancia
que al descubrirte me gané el derecho
de salir cada noche
a mirar tu expresiva luz errante,
tu joven brillantez inmaculada,
sin tener ni la mínima esperanza
de estrechar tu verdad entre mis brazos.

Te inventé con la alquimia de mis sueños
te vestí de imposible,
en tus pupilas inicié un poema
y en lo más alto entronicé tu imagen.

Con barro de mi angustia te di forma
igual a la de un ángel que no existe.

Nocturne: Alchemy of My Dreams

I love you as if you were a star.
I dare to contemplate your brightness
to feel your luminous purity,
to climb the heights where you appear
with my yearnings
but never to touch you
nor place my caresses
on the brilliant skin of your mystery.

I know where you appear each day.
I know the exact spot
and the precise hour
when your face shows its beauty.
I know your celestial orbit
by heart
that glorious instant
when you shine closest to my eyes
and also the moment
you leave and steal away your likeness.

I know I am your owner from afar,
that when I discovered you I won the right
to come out each night
to watch your expressive, errant light,
your immaculate, brilliant youth,
without the least hope
of embracing the truth of you in my arms.

I invented you with the alchemy of my dreams.
I dressed you with the impossible.
In your eyes I began a poem
and I enthroned your image on high.

I gave you form with the clay of my anguish
like that of an angel who doesn't exist.

Cuando llega la noche
y te encuentro rielando en el espacio:
yo te aspiro y te gozo,
platico desde lejos con tu nimbo
sin pronunciar tu nombre.
Sin esperar tampoco que desciendas
ni que el roce de mi tacto te defina:
porque anhelo que ignoren mis sentidos
que eres de carne y hueso,
que tu cuerpo es mortal,
y que hasta el nítido esplendor que irradias,
carece de luz propia.

¡Sigue alumbrando allá! ¡Brilla unos días!
Pronto la muerte bajará mis párpados
y tú, al instante, quedarás a oscuras.

Eternidad del polvo
1970

When night comes
and I find you glistening in space
I want you and desire you.
I talk with your halo from far away
without speaking your name,
without hoping that you might descend,
or define you with the gaze of my touch.
I long for my senses to become numb
that you are flesh and blood
that your being is mortal
and that the splendor you radiate
caresses light itself.

Keep shining! Shine a few more days!
Soon death will lower my eyelids —
and suddenly you will be left in the dark.

Tengo miedo

Tengo miedo de ti,
de mí,
del mundo, del aire,
del amor, de la sombra.
Tengo miedo de todo.
¡Tengo miedo del miedo!
Tengo miedo de caer
sin nombre,
sin memoria y sin cuerpo,
en la eternidad
del olvido y del silencio.

¿Para qué soy
si para siempre dejaré de
serlo?

Eternidad del polvo
1970

¿Qué es morir?

— Morir es
alzar el vuelo
sin alas
sin ojos
y sin cuerpo.

Eternidad del polvo
1970

132

I Am Afraid

I am afraid of you
of me,
of the world, of air,
of love, of shade.
I am afraid of everything.
I am afraid of fear!
I am afraid of falling
into the eternity
of oblivion and silence
without a name
without memory or body.

What am I good for
if I am afraid
of being it?

What Is Dying?

To die is
to take flight
without wings
without eyes
and without body.

133

Diálogo en sombras

Cuando del sueño despierto
en mi lecho oscurecido
y soy silencio tendido
por la soledad cubierto;

cuando la noche es desierto
por volátil sombra henchido
y la ausencia del sonido
deambula su idioma muerto:

descubro que, cauteloso,
mi pensamiento se vierte
en el orbe del reposo

y, mi vigilia convierte
en un diálogo amoroso
que sostengo con mi muerte...

Eternidad del polvo
1970

Dialogue in Shadows

When I wake up from dreaming
on my darkened bed
attended by silence
covered by solitude

when the night is desert
filled by volatile shadows
and the absence of sound
rambles its dead language

I cautiously discover that
my thoughts empty themselves
into the orb of rest

and my vigil becomes
a loving dialogue
I maintain with my death...

Poema a mi dios

Ni símbolo, ni juez,
ni forma yerta,
es el Dios potencial que me imagino:
porque el mío
—¡verdad de lo divino!—
existe y late como fuerza cierta.

Yo siento que es la entraña
de la abierta corola universal,
y lo adivino
lo mismo en el relámpago asesino
que en la luz que del astro se deserta.

Es imposible atesorar
lo inmenso
— la esencia sin final y sin comienzo —
en patética forma dolorida.

¡Dios es eternidad!
y su presencia
abarca desde el cielo a mi conciencia,
y Él es Todo,
y yo parte de su vida.

Eternidad del polvo
1970

Poem to My God

The god that I imagine
is neither symbol, nor judge,
nor fixed statue
because mine
— truly divine —
exists and exerts real force.

I feel he is the center
of an open, universal blossom
and I imagine him
like anihilating lightning
lost in the light of a star.

It is impossible to hoard
the immense
— the essence without end or beginning —
in a sad, sorrowful form.

God is eternity
and his presence
reaches from the sky to my conscience.
He is Everything
and I part of his life!

Poema de mi fe

Es que no necesito de dogmas religiosos
para creer en Dios.

Estoy convencido
de que existe. Y no porque capte
algún sentido de mi cuerpo
el roce de sus tactos misteriosos,
ni tampoco porque lo invente
en los peligrosos instantes
para darme valor. Si yo he creído,
es porque lo escucho hablar en mi entraña,
escondido en el mar de mi sangre,
dictándome amoroso
con una voz inmensa que parece fundirse
con mi propio silencio,
en íntima armonía:
el poema desnudo que no puede decirse
porque no hay palabras que den su profecía.

Y por este poema
que, aunque no puede asirse,
me circula por dentro,
creo de Dios: ¡POESIA!

Eternidad del polvo
1970

Poem of My Faith

I don't need religious dogmas
to believe in God.

I'm convinced
he exists. And not because
some physical sense
feels his mysterious touch,
or because I invented him
to give me strength
in time of danger. If I've believed
it's because I hear him inside me,
hidden in the ocean of my blood,
speaking to me lovingly
with an immense voice that seems fused
in intimate harmony
with my own silence:
the naked poem I cannot speak
because there are no words to give it voice.

Although it cannot be grasped,
through this poem
circulating inside of me,
I believe in God: Poetry!

Dentro de mí

Con los ojos
altamente asomados a la noche
contemplo las estrellas
y dentro de mí,
en el río incansable de mi sangre,
las siento y las descubro
reflejadas,
luminosas y hondas,
como si mi entraña fuera
el mismo cielo
en donde están ardiendo.

Eternidad del polvo
1970

Inside of Me

With my eyes
wide open to the night
I contemplate the stars.
Inside of me,
in the ceaseless river of my blood,
I feel them and discover them
reflected
luminous and deep
as if my insides were
the same sky
where they are burning.

Perfección fugaz

Pinté el tallo,
luego el cáliz,
después la corola
pétalo por pétalo,
y,
al terminar mi rosa,
la induje
a sonar su aroma.

¡Hice la rosa perfecta!

Tan perfecta
que al día siguiente,
cuando fui a mirarla,

ya estaba muerta.

Cerca de lo lejos
1979

Fleeting Perfection

I painted the stem,
then the base
followed by the inner leaves,
petal by petal
and
when I finished my rose
I encouraged it
to dream its scent.

I created the perfect rose!

So perfect that,
when I went to admire it,
the next day

it was already withered.

Casi a la orilla

Después de lo gozado y lo sufrido,
después de lo ganado y lo perdido,
siento que existo aun porque ya,
casi a la orilla de mi vida,
puedo recordar y gozar
enloquecido: en lo que he sido,
en lo que es ido...

Cerca de lo lejos
1979

Pre-Meditación

Cuando me llevaron a confesar
por primera vez,
le dije al sacerdote
todos mis pecados...
Pero menos uno
que pensaba cometer después.

Cerca de lo lejos
1979

Almost to the Shore

After what's been enjoyed and endured
after what's been lost and won
I feel I still exist because
I am almost to the other shore, already
going on senile, I remember and enjoy:
what I have been
what is now gone...

Pre-Meditated

When they took me to confession
for the first time,
I told the priest
all my sins...
Except one
I was thinking of committing later.

El poema inasible

Traigo entre ceja y ceja
un poema
que en las noches escribo
por detrás de mis párpados,
y se borra en el día
cuando los abro.

Igual que las estrellas
resplandece en desnudez
cuando la sombra impera,
y se apaga
cuando la luz lo invade.

Me lo sé de memoria
sin saber lo que dice;
porque es un poema
que, por más que lo escribo
por detrás de mis parpados,
jamás he podido

concretarlo en palabras.
Yo tengo la esperanza
de que, cuando me ausente,
algún poeta anónimo
lo capte entre su sueño
y, al despertar, lo haga.

*(Es el poema eterno
que a todos los poetas
se nos esconde adentro
sin poderlo decir.
El que nos sobrevive
en el pulso del aire
esperando que alguien
lo descubra, lo entienda
y lo quiera escribir.)*

Cerca de lo lejos
1979

Out-of-Reach Poem

Between eyebrow and eyebrow
I carry a poem
I write at night
behind my eyelids
and I erase it each day
when I open them.

Like the stars
resplendent, unadorned
when shadows reign,
it disappears
when light invades.

I know it by heart
without knowing what it says
because it's a poem
I write
behind my eyelids,
but am able unable

to put it in words.
I live with the hope
that when I am gone
some anonymous poet
will capture it in his dream
and write it down on waking.

(It is the eternal poem
hiding inside
all poets
but they cannot express it—
the one that survives us
in the pulse of air
waiting for someone
to discover it, understand it,
and want to write it.)

Meteoro

Sobre la mesa
un vaso
se desmaya,
          rueda,
          cae.

Al estrellarse
contra el piso,
una galaxia
          nace.

Cerca de lo lejos
1979

Cuando las campanas

En mi pueblo, al oscurecer,
cuando las campanas
dan el toque de oración
las gentes en plena calle
se arrodillan,
se persignan,
cierran los ojos
y, sin saber por qué,
ni de qué, piden perdón...

(La pobreza es su pecado,
y el infierno su temor.)

Cerca de lo lejos
1979

Meteor

On the table
a glass
faints,
     rolls,
     falls.

When it crashes
against the floor,
a galaxy
     is born.

When the Bells

In my hometown, at nightfall,
when the bells
toll the time to pray
people kneel
in the middle of the street
bless themselves,
close their eyes,
and beg forgiveness
without knowing why or from what...

(Poverty is their sin,
and hell their fear.)

Derecho de propiedad

¡Nada es tan mío
como lo es el mar
cuando lo miro!

Cerca de lo lejos
1979

Eternidad carnal

Vámonos quedando así
como los perros, pegados,
hasta que venga la muerte
a separarnos.
O que nos sepulten juntos
ensartados como estamos.
¡Qué más da que difuntos
sigamos cohabitando
bajo tierra, mortalmente enamorados!

Erotismo al rojo blanco
1983

Property Rights

Nothing is more mine
than the sea
when I gaze out on it.

Sexual Eternity

Let's stay this way,
like two dogs, stuck together,
until death comes
to separate us.
Let them bury us together
skewered like this.
Who cares if we're dead,
still together underground
mortally in love!

Nocturno a tientas

A oscuras, yacentes
en el mismo lecho,
somos brasas despiertas
que vigilan
el pulso de sus lumbres.

Me animo y aventuro
mi mano por su cuerpo:
voy encontrando
laderas y llanuras,
asomo de pezones
y un par
de lomas redondas
que un precipicio
aparta
haciendo entre las dos
una cañada.

A tientas
en su fondo palpo
un inasible vello
casi sueño..
parece que ando cerca
de las puertas del cielo.

El merodeo prosigue
y después
de subidas y bajadas,
bajadas y subidas,
doy con algo
inédito y matrero.
— Hallazgo afortunado
que al fin me queda
como anillo al dedo.

Erotismo al rojo blanco
1983

Nocturne: Groping

In the dark, lying
in the same bed,
we are live coals
wide awake, vigilant
to the pulse of their burning.

Excited, I venture
my hand along your body:
I travel finding
flatlands and slopes,
nipples appear
and a pair
of rounded hills
separated
by a precipice
creating a gorge
between them.

Groping
in the depths I touch
soft, downy hair
almost dreamlike...
as if leading me
to the gates of heaven.

The pillaging continues
and then,
climbing and descending,
descending and climbing,
I find something
bashful and cunning.
— What good fortune
that in the end I find
it fits like a ring on my finger.

Pinche orgullo

No puedo dormir
porque no estoy en mí,
sino contigo, en tu casa
y los dos desnudos
en la misma cama.

Y también tú,
en estos momentos
debes estar
siendo lo mismo,
porque no estás en tí,
sino aquí conmigo,
en esta hoguera
de soledad y sábanas
donde forcejeo
con el rebelde cuerpo
de tu ausencia.

Por el terco *amor propio*,
por este pinche orgullo
estamos separados
en diferentes lechos,
desabrazados
y abrasados
por idénticos infiernos,
en los que, los dos quizá
desvistiendo y mordiendo
las almohadas,
logremos mitigar
en esta noche larga,
el hambre dolorosa de los sexos
y las llamas heladas de este fuego.

Erotismo al rojo blanco
1983

154

Damned Pride

I cannot sleep
because I am not in me
but with you, in your house
and both of us naked
in the same bed.

And you too
at this moment
must be
feeling the same,
because you are not in you,
but here with me,
in this bonfire
of solitude and sheets
where I struggle
with the rebellious body
of your absence.

Because of stubborn selfishness,
because of damned pride,
we are separated
in different beds
not embracing
but embraced
by identical hell-fires
where both of us, perhaps
undressed and biting
the pillows
through the long night,
manage to lessen
the sad hunger of it
and the frozen flames of this fire.

Aclaración

El pecado se comete
al no cometerlo
y, si estás en pecado
no entrarás al cielo.
Reflexiona. Yo pienso
que hacerlo, es lo mejor.
Así estaremos a salvo
del infierno, los dos.

Erotismo al rojo blanco
1983

Clarification

Sin is committed sometimes
by not doing something
and, if you are in sin,
you will not enter heaven.
Think about it. Perhaps
it is better that we do it.
That way both of us
will be saved from hell.

Hay veces que salimos

Hay veces que salimos
a entrar en la caverna de la noche,
con la carga senil de tantos años
y la helada impotencia
del floripondio flácido,
sin poder, sin deseo, manojo inerte;
pero que el vicio enerva
y el recuerdo revive,
haciendo que nos duela
como hielo pegado entre las ingles.

Hay veces que ya, fatigados, desistimos
de ambular y ambular por la penumbra,
o de ver los espasmos que arrancamos
al cruzar las luces de los bares
o el azote instantáneo de los faros
de los automóviles errantes,
y regresamos solos,
con una soledad de luto amargo
que con reseca humedad
debajo de la ropa se desliza
como contacto de algún tacto frío
y llegamos por fin a desvestirnos
a tendernos de nuevo en nuestros lechos
más solos que antes de salir
incitados por el deseo de la aventura.

Ya tendidos buscamos el consuelo
inoperante de una masturbación que sin final
termina por dormirnos.

sin fecha
Elías Nandino revisitado
2002

Sometimes When We Go Out

Sometimes when we go out
to enter the cavern of night
with the senile burden of so many years
and the frozen impotence
of that flaccid flourish,
un-aroused a lifeless handful;
but vice energizes us
and memory revives us,
making us ache
like ice stuck between our legs.

Sometimes, abandoned and tired
of walking and walking through shadows,
of seeing the spasms we create
walking in front of the lights of the bars
or the sudden flashes of headlights
coming and going,
we return alone,
with a solitude of bitter mourning
with parched sweat
melting beneath our clothing
like contact with some cold touch
and finally we get undressed,
lie down in our beds again
roused by this desire for adventure
more alone now than before we went out.

Lying back, we settle for the empty consolation
of an unsatisfying masturbation which finally ends
when we fall asleep.

no date

159

Las iguanas

Son las iguanas
animales extáticos
que, sobre las rocas
al contemplar el sol
adivinan a Dios.

Banquete íntimo
1993

Luciérnagas

La tarde expira
la oscuridad comienza:
sólo se miran
los súbitos haikais
que escriben las luciérnagas.

Banquete íntimo
1993

The Iguanas

The iguanas are
animals of ecstasy
who contemplate the sun
from the rocks,
trying to understand God.

Fireflies

The afternoon fades,
darkness begins.
All you can see
are the sudden haiku
composed by the fireflies.

El eclipse

Ver un eclipse
a todos nos convence
que Dios existe
y que se mueve su Cosmos
con pericia infalible.

Banquete íntimo
1993

Pradera de haikais
(Fragment)

XIII

¡Hay luna llena
busca papel y lápiz
y haz un poema!

Banquete íntimo
1993

The Eclipse

To see an eclipse,
everyone is convinced
that God exists
and his Cosmos moves
with infallible order.

A Meadow of Haiku
(Fragment)

13

See there a full moon.
Search for paper and pencil.
Then write a poem!

En una noche

En plena noche
capturé una luciérnaga
— chispa furtiva —.
Al buscarla en mi mano
sólo era poesía.

Banquete íntimo
1993

Con la sonrisa

Con la sonrisa
y la mirada
el niño inventa otra
palabra.
Aprehéndela
en tu poema
con invisible
tinta mágica.

sin fecha
Elías Nandino revisitado
2000

One Night

In the darkest of night
I caught a firefly
— furtive spark.
When I looked in my hand
there was a poem.

With a Smile

With a smile
and a look
the child invents
a word.
Catch it
with invisible
magic ink
in your poem.

no date

Algún día

Como no llueve
la tierra está reseca
y el polvo vuela:
(Algún día volaremos
como esta tierra ciega.)

Banquete íntimo,
1993

Someday

Without any rain,
the earth is parched
and the dust is flying:
(Someday we will fly
like this blind dust.)

Bibliography

Works by Elías Nandino

Poetry

Banquete íntimo. Guadalajara: Secretaría de Cultura de Jalisco. 1993.
Canciones (1915–1919), in *Poesía I*. Privately printed, 1947.
Cerca de lo lejos, Poesía 1972–1978. México, DF: Fondo de Cultura Económica, Letras mexicanas, 1979.
Ciclos terrenales, Poesía 1979–1989. México, DF: Plaza y Valdés, 1989.
Color de ausencia (1919–1924). Privately printed, 1932.
Conversación con el mar y otras poemas (1947) in *Poesía II*. México, DF: Nueva Voz, 1948.
Conversación con mi muerte (1947), in *Poesía II*. México, DF: Nueva Voz, 1948.
Eco (1934). Prologue by Xavier Villaurutia, México, DF: Imprenta Mundial, 1934.
Erotismo al rojo blanco. México, DF: Editorial Domés, 1983.
Espejo de mi muerte. México, DF: Manuel Altoaguirre Impresor, 1945.
Espiral (1924–1928). Privately printed, 1928.
Eternidad del polvo. México, DF: Joaquín Mortiz, Las Dos Orillas, 1970.
Naufragio de la duda. México, DF: Nueva Voz, 1950.
Nocturna palabra. México, DF: Fondo de Cultura Económico, 1960.
Nocturna suma. DF: México, DF: Tezontle, 1955.
Nocturno día. México, DF: Editorial Estaciones, 1959.
Nudo de sombras (1941), in *Poesía I*. Privately printed, 1947.
Poemas árboles. México, DF: Ediciones Norte, 1938.
Prismas de sangre (1945), in *Poesía II*. México, DF: Nueva Voz, 1948.
Rio de sombra (1935). México, DF: Imprenta Mundial, 1935.
Sonetos (nuevos 1939), in *Sonetos 1937–1939*. México, DF: Editorial Katún, 1983.
Sonetos. México, DF: privately printed, 1937.
Suicidio lento. México, FD: Chápero, 1937.
Triangulos de silencios. México, DF: Guaraní, Coleccíon Nezahualcóyotl, 1953.

Fiction

El coronelito. Guadalajara: Editorial Ágata, 1991.

Autobiography

Juntando mis pasos. México, DF: Editorial Aldus, 2000.

Compilations and Anthologies

Antología poetica, 1924–1982. Selected and with prologue by Sandro Cohen. México, DF: Editorial Dónes. 1983.

Costumbre de morir a diario: Siete Nocturnos. Selected by Jorge Esquinca. Prologue by Xavier Villaurrutía. Guadalajara: Departmento de Bellas Artes y FONA-PAS. 1982.

Décimas en la muerte de mi madre y otras poemas. México, DF: Nueva Voz, 1966.

Dos poemarios afines ... de siglo. Guadalajara: Editorial Ágata, 1993.

Elías Nandino de bolsillo. Guadalajara: Universidad de Guadalajara, 1990.

Elías Nandino para jóvenes. México, DF: Consejo Nacional para la Cultura y las Artes, Instituto de Bellas Artes. 1990.

Elías Nandino: El azul es el verde que se aleja. Selección, prólogo y notas de Jorge Esquinca. Guadalajara: Secretaría de Cultura — Gobierno de Jalisco. 2008.

En los cabellos del árbol. México, DF: Consejo Nacional para la Culura y las Artes, 2001.

La noche y la poesía. México, DF: Consejo Nacional para la Cultura y las Artes, Instituto Nacional de Bellas Artes, 1992.

Medio rostro de una vida, Poesia 1916–1948. Guadalajara: Editorial Donés, 1981.

Nocturnos intemporales. México, DF: Universidad Autónoma Metropolitana, 1990.

Poesia I, (1924–1945) Privately Printed, 1947.

Poesia II, (1945–1948). México, DF: Nueva Voz, 1948.

Poesía selecta. México, DF: Editorial Katún. 1982.

Sonetos de amor 1937–1939. Guadalajara: Ediciones Colegio Internacional. 1973.

Todos mis nocturnos. Guadalajara: Ayuntamiento de Guadalajara. 1988.

Works About Elías Nandino

Books

Aguilar, Enrique. *Elías Nandino: una vida no/velada*. México, DF: Océano, 2000.

Encarnación, Salvador. *Elías Nandino revisitado*. Hojas Literarias, Serie Poesía 47. Guadalajara, Jalisco: Secretaría de Cultura de Jalisco, 2000.

Gutiérrez López, Gabriela. *Elías Nandino*. Hojas Literarias, Serie Ensayo 23. Guadalajara, Jalisco: Secretaría de Cultura de Jalisco, 2000.

Saavedra García, Mario. *Elías Nandino: Poeta de la vida, poeta de la muerte*. Guadalajaara, Jalisco: Ediotorial Agata, 1997.

Introductions, Prefaces, Forewords

Cohen, Sandro. "Prólogo: Elías Nandino en el balance." *Elías Nandino: Antologia Poética 1924–1982*. México, DF: Editorial Donés, 1983. 11–26.

Esquinca, Jorge. "Introducción." *Elías Nandino: Costumbre de morir a diario: Siete Nocturnos.* Guadalajara, Jalisco: Departamento de Bellas Artes, Gobierno de Jalisco. 1984. 3–6.

Monsivais, Carlos. "De los poderes menguantes y las recuperaciones irónicas." *Erotismo al rojo vivo.* By Nandino. Guadalajara, Jalisco, México: Editorial Agata, 1991.

Montemayor, Carlos. "Presentación: El nocturno en Elías Nandino." *Eternidad del polvo/Nocturna palabra.* By Nandino. Tercera Serie 43, Lecturas Mexicanas. México, DF: Consejo Nacional para la Cultura y las Artes, 1991. 11–20.

Chapters, Articles and Publications in Periodicals

Canton, Wilberto. "Elías Nandino." *Letras vivas: Páginas de la literatura mexicana actual.* México, DF: Secretaría de Educación Pública, 1972. 107–136.

Cárdenas de la Peña, Enrique. "Tres poetas médicos de la era moderna." *Anales Médicos* 51 : 84–89.

Carter, Boyd. "Elías Nandino y la revista 'Estaciones.'" *Hispania* 45, (1962): 78–80.

Castro, José Alberto. "Las memorias de Nandino." *Proceso,* 4 de julio 2000 : 95.

Dausster, Frank. "Triunfo de la duda: La poesía de Elías Nandino" *Ensayos sobre poesía mexicana.* Colección Stadium-412. México, DF : Ediciones de Andrea, 1963. 52–73.

Ellis, Robert Richmond. "Elías Nandino and Raúl Thomas: Writing in and out of Machismo." *They Dream Not of Angels but of Men.* Gainsville: Univeristy Press of Florida, 2002. 101–123.

Forster, Merlin H. "El grupo." *Los contemporaneos 1920–1932: Perfil de un experimento vanguardista mexicano.* Mexico, DF: Ediciones Andrea, 1964. 11–23.

Gutiérrez, Gabriela. "Elías Nandino." *Revista de la Universidad Nacional Autónoma de México* 53 (1998) : 60–63.

Montiel, Elise L. "Elias Nandino, a poet of vitality and talent." *Voices of Mexico* 26, (1994) : 37–39.

Pérez de Mendiola, Marina. "Nandino, Elías" in *Latin American Writers on Gay and Lesbian Themes: A Bio-critical Sourcebook.* Ed. David William Foster. Westport, Connecticut: Greenwood Press, 1994. 281–286.

Taggart, Kenneth M. "Nandino, Elias." *Dictionary of Mexican Literature.* Ed. Eladio Cortes. Westport, Connecticut: Greenwood Press, 1992. 454.

Vazquez Amaral, José. "A literary letter from Mexico." *New York Times,* Sept. 16, 1956, BR23.

Verdugo Fuentes, Waldemar. "Elías Nandino." *Páginas para la historia.* México, DF: Universidad Autónoma del Estado de México, 1988, March 23, 2005 <http://www.galeon.com/entrevistas2/familia779141.html>.

Index

173